United States
Department
of Agriculture

Forest Service

Rocky Mountain
Research Station

General Technical
Report RMRS-GTR-177

September 2006

Wood Plenty, Grass Good, Water None

Vegetation Changes in Arizona's Upper Verde River Watershed From 1850 to 1997

Harley G. Shaw

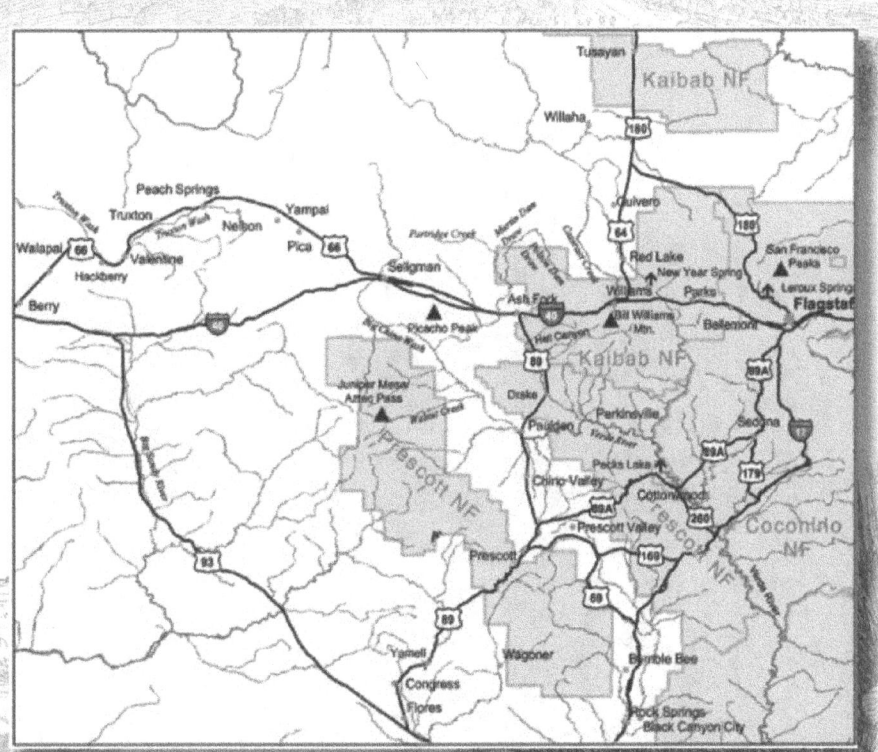

Shaw, Harley G. 2006. **Wood plenty, grass good, water none: Vegetation changes in Arizona's upper Verde River watershed from 1850 to 1997.** Gen. Tech. Rep. RMRS-GTR-177. Fort Collins, CO: U.S. Department of Agriculture, Forest Service, Rocky Mountain Research Station. 50 p.

Abstract—The purpose of this study was to compare current woodland density and distribution in and around the dry upper Verde River watershed in northwestern Arizona with conditions prior to Anglo settlement. Historic conditions were assessed using early photographs and early diaries and reports. The expedition led by Amiel Weeks Whipple was retraced and areas described in 1854 compared with the present. Diaries and reports of members of the Sitgreaves (1851) and Ives (1858) expeditions, Francis Aubry (1857), Edward Beale, John Marion (1870), and Edgar Mearns were also used to assess presettlement woodland conditions. Photographs from 1867, 1871, 1910, and 1917 were repeated between 1995 and 1999. Based upon these early sources, I hypothesize that the aerial distribution of woodlands have not changed greatly since 1851, although densities within many stands have increased. I conclude that at least three dense stands of woodland of unknown extent existed in the study area as early as 1851.

Key words: Vegetation history, woodlands, juniper, Topographical Engineers, Army Explorations, Verde River watershed, Arizona, Whipple, Sitgreaves, Ives, Mearns

The Author

Harley Shaw is a retired wildlife research biologist. He completed a B.S. in Wildlife Management at the University of Arizona and an M.S. in Wildlife Management at the University of Idaho. He worked for Arizona Game and Fish Department for 27 years.

Wood Plenty, Grass Good, Water None

Vegetation Changes in Arizona's Upper Verde River Watershed From 1850 to 1997

Harley G. Shaw

United States Department of Agriculture
Forest Service
Rocky Mountain Research Station

Preface and Acknowledgments

The first government-supported expeditions through northern Arizona—those led by Sitgreaves, Whipple, Ives, and Beale—used horses, mules, and in Whipple's case, equine-drawn wagons, to traverse the area. Beale experimented with camels but also used equines. While these parties had definite routes that they wanted to explore, their travel was much controlled by terrain and the availability of water and grass for livestock. They traveled in the cooler months hoping to reduce the need for water, the most critical requirement. As a result of fall, winter, or early spring travel, they arrived in the high country of the Southwest when nights were inevitably cold, and winter storms could make life miserable for days at a stretch. Thus, a third item, wood for fires, became important. In addition, all of these explorations were made with an eye to future settlement, to wagon or railroad routes, raising of cattle, and farming potential. Any such enterprises required wood, water, and grass, and these elements appear in the various diaries in a virtual rhythm. The last daily entry for many of the diarists was a notation describing the availability of wood, grass, and water. Thus the title of this report.

The work reported here was carried out mostly as a "hobby" project. I received limited funding from two foundations, mainly to help locate and acquire copies of historic photographs. The Chino Valley District of the U.S. Forest Service provided some help with photo processing and vehicle expenses, strictly on a cost-share basis. As a result, I must present the report for what it is: a limited effort by an interested individual to document conditions in the woodlands just before and during Anglo settlement, which includes my own photographs and observations regarding conditions in these same woodlands during the 1990s. I have now moved away from the area of study and on to other interests. As a result, I am unlikely to fill any of the gaps that may exist. I have tried to remove unwarranted conclusions or speculations regarding pre- or post-settlement anthropogenic or climatic effects. I assume that anyone studying vegetation history in the area would want to delve into historic photos and journals, and I hope that this manuscript might save them time.

Unraveling the various routes taken by separate parties of the Whipple expedition has been a challenge. Presenting them in a way that is easy to understand, even more challenging. I have tried to clearly separate the travels of Whipple's three reconnaissance excursions from the more restricted travels of the larger wagon train. If alternating between the two remains confusing, I can only apologize. I haven't come up with anything better. Another source of potential confusion lies in my use, at times, of Whipple's itinerary as published in the Railroad Survey Report and in his handwritten diary. Whipple presented his itinerary as if it were copied directly from his diary, but it had in fact been modified in many places when his official report was being prepared. The actual diary helps to clarify some points and, at times, provides better descriptions of the landscapes. In quoting all of the various diaries, I've retained the spelling and punctuation of the diarists.

Rather than clutter the text with parenthetical binomials where various species are mentioned, I provided a list in Appendix D. I used the PLANTS database (http://plants.usda.gov/) for plant names, Wilson and Reeder (http://nmnhgoph.si.edu/msw/) for mammals, and the American Ornithologist's Union Bird List (http://www.aou.org/aou/birdlist.html) for birds.

Although I try to avoid conclusions regarding the importance of various factors affecting the woodlands in the area of interest, I have, rather to my surprise, developed one hypotheses and one conclusion regarding presettlement conditions as compared with the present. First, I believe the evidence presented here suggests strongly that the distribution of woodlands over the area is not much different now than it was in the 1850s. Second, while overall juniper density may have been lower prior to Anglo settlement, at least three areas clearly were covered with very dense woodlands. One area, Polson Dam Draw northeast of Ash Fork, may have had a denser stand of juniper in the 1850s than it does now. Another, north of Walnut Creek and including a portion of Juniper Mesa may have lost junipers between the 1850s and 1916 and then returned to high densities later.

This work was initiated under grants from the Margaret T. Morris Foundation and a second anonymous foundation, which paid for the initial searches for historic photographs and covered expenses of many of the rephotography trips. These foundations also funded publication of a catalog of early photographs (Shaw and McCroskey 1995). The Prescott National Forest supplemented the above funds with a cost-share grant for fieldwork. Individuals who helped with fieldwork or other aspects of the job include Shawn Bower, Gray Bower, Peter Janknecht, Sue Schuhardt, Tom and Marge Perkins, David and Christine Coblentz, Mike Wurtz, Warren Miller, Janet Lovelady, Richard Sims, and Jay Eby. Raymond M. Turner spent three days in the field with me, checking some of my early photograph relocations and providing large format repeat photographs of the sites. Dr. Turner also reviewed in detail an early draft of the manuscript. An anonymous reviewer critiqued an earlier version of this manuscript, and his comments have been incorporated. Other reviewers include David Brown, Patrick Boles, Robert Euler, Arlan Helgeson, Tom Jonas, Al Medina, Carolyn Sieg, and Andrew Wallace. Dr. Peter Janknecht of Braga, Portugal spent time with me in the woodlands of northern Arizona and willingly interpreted the Möllhausen manuscript from the Ives expedition from German into English. His knowledge of the area has been invaluable in assessing the finer connotations of some of the German words. Eugene P. Polk provided comment and encouragement along the way. Bruce Fee alerted me to the Sherburn manuscript and provided a copy. Patty Woodruff listened to my constant theorizing, has read and re-read the manuscript, and added her eyes and ears, as well as her companionship, to my days afield.

Contents

Wood Plenty, Grass Good, Water None

Vegetation Changes in Arizona's Upper Verde River Watershed From 1850 to 1997

Harley G. Shaw

Introduction_____

Many ranchers and resource managers have noted that piñon and juniper invaded large expanses of historic grassland in northern Arizona over the past 150 years (Arnold and others. 1964; Johnsen 1962). Since the time of European arrival in Arizona, woodlands have constantly been cut or cleared for a variety of reasons. Early fuelwooding and post-cutting, associated with ranching, mining, and railroads, eliminated most of the larger trees. Later, chaining, cutting, bulldozing, and burning for the sole purpose of clearing trees to favor grasses were attempted with varied success. Few people described juniper forests as they existed prior to the arrival of livestock and railroads. Until recently, no one systematically monitored the cleared areas after trees were removed.

Over the past 25 years, studies of prehistory of vegetation (Betancourt and others 1990; Anderson, 1989) have provided new understanding of post-Pleistocene changes in plant distribution in the Southwest, which resulted mainly from changing continental climate. Studies of prehistoric vegetation provide a backdrop for measuring more recent change, but the tools used do not provide resolution fine enough to assess changes in limited areas over the past 150 years, a period concurrent with Anglo expansion into the Southwest. We know little of the densities of woodlands that existed on and around the upper Verde River watershed when the first settlers arrived in the 1860s, and much of the early clearing of junipers had been accomplished before anyone began to study the history of plant communities. Most of the existing records represent conditions that developed after the initial clearing of junipers; heavy grazing of grasslands had already occurred as well.

A current philosophy of wildland management encourages foresters to re-create pre-settlement conditions. Yet these conditions are not easily defined. We know that change in the environment was happening before the earliest humans arrived in North America at the end of the Pleistocene, and it has continued with varying degrees of human influence both before and after modern settlement. Fire, freezing, drought, floods, along with global climatic variation, modify vegetation patterns. At times, these changes may be drastic and rapid: a flood removes riparian vegetation along a stream or wildfire eliminates a mature stand of trees. Between such catastrophic events, the mosaic of vegetation changes shifts subtly with long-term fluctuations in precipitation, temperature, and agents of seed dispersal.

Thus, any perception of "original conditions" at any given site are dependent upon the time in history when a particular observer entered the scene. Early Anglo settlers did not reflect upon landscape ecology, and such subjects as fire history, plant succession, and woodland demographics were not of concern. Owning the land, making a living, and growing rich, dominated their thoughts. Few carried cameras, and when they did, they mostly photographed other people. If they shot landscapes, they were usually of the grandiose and extreme, or of human settlements. Only a few kept diaries, mainly noting adventures and difficulties, hence their descriptions of vegetation were rare and brief. For most of them, the wilderness was something to be subdued; they had no reason to think of vegetation as a part of history.

Many questions therefore remain unanswered regarding vegetation change in northern Arizona. How much change has really happened in the grassland/piñon-juniper communities since Anglos arrived? How have the boundaries between woodland and grassland moved? How stable are they? How pervasive is the change in distribution of trees or shrubs? What were the original densities of woody vegetation? What was the timing of change? Did it occur rapidly following some single event—either natural or human-caused? Or is this an intrinsic pattern that may be only partly influenced by humans? What was the presettlement composition of the grasslands and understory vegetation within the woodlands?

The use of diaries and old photographs to view historic habitats provides one method of approaching these questions (Hastings and Turner 1965; Bahre 1991). Such sources give glimpses of the landscapes that existed immediately prior to, during, and since, settlement. Their use also leave many questions unanswered. They show us only the beginning and the present but little of what happened in between. They tell us little about early conditions regarding herbaceous or ephemeral plants.

Grazing by domestic livestock has been blamed for woodland encroachment on grasslands more than any other factor. That the sudden arrival of large numbers of ungulates could create change seems reasonable, especially if the area had previously been free of grazers. Grazing is a persistent, visible land use, hence easy to indict. But the intensity and time of grazing itself must be considered. Moderate, well managed grazing may create little if any change. Conversely, an event of extremely heavy grazing over a relatively short period, perhaps a decade or less, can permanently change a landscape, regardless of subsequent treatment. Other activities, such as the cutting of fuel wood for railroads and mines at the end of the last century, happen quickly and are easily forgotten. They too, may set ecological processes into motion that continue indefinitely. A problem exists in separating changes that would have happened regardless of human impacts and those that were truly caused by postsettlement activities.

Fire is an important factor that falls within this second category. Fire frequency may have changed drastically due to reduced fuels on heavily grazed lands and of direct fire prevention efforts by land management agencies. The changes in fire frequency have been well-documented for forested areas at higher elevations in the Southwest (Swetnam and Baisan 1996). They are less understood for woodlands, especially pure juniper woodlands. This is in part because aging junipers with dendrochronological methods is more difficult than aging pine species. It is also partly because juniper does not sustain fire scars well and, in fact, often dies when subjected to fire. Evidence to date suggests that large fire frequency and replacement periods are much longer in woodlands than in forests (Floyd and others 2000).

Uncertainty exists regarding northern Arizona's pre-grazing conditions. Some early writers suggest that the grasslands were originally more lush than they are today. One often-quoted statement, attributed to Charles Genung, an early settler of Skull Valley, proclaimed that grasses were tall enough to hide a horse (Hall 1934). While such stands might have existed in wetlands, they probably were not characteristic of the drier uplands. Certainly none of the presettlement photographs of the Plains and Great Basin Grasslands lend credence to such growth, and early diaries suggest that conditions were austere at best. Differences in observations may reflect annual or seasonal variations in precipitation, hence temporary vegetation conditions seen by different travelers at different times.

Early differences in descriptions of the landscape may also reflect the backgrounds, attitudes, and expectations of the observers. Many of the early diarists grew up in the forests of the eastern United States. While they might find the open stands of mature ponderosa pine forests on the Mogollon Rim imposing, they were probably not impressed with our southwestern oaks and "cedars," compared with oak or red cedar forests of the East. Similarly, the short, sparse stands of grama grass in the Southwest were not particularly noteworthy compared with eastern savannas or tall grass prairie.

Study Area

I focused mainly on the upper Verde River watershed, roughly from Bill Williams Mountain to the east, the head of Partridge Creek to the north, Aztec Pass to the west, and Walnut Creek where it enters Big Chino Valley to the south. The upper Verde River watershed was one of the last areas in the continental United States to be settled by Europeans when the 1850s military expeditions set the stage for settlement in the area.

The study area (fig. 1) encompasses the routes explored and described by Army Topographical Engineers Sitgreaves, Whipple, Ives, and Beale during the 1850s. I used the routes described by the various expeditions as historic vegetation "transects." I emphasized that portion of the Whipple expedition between New Year Spring northeast of Bill Williams Mountain and Aztec Pass at the head of Walnut Creek because of the greater amount of information recorded by the members of the Whipple party. This route crosses much of the "dry" upper part of the Verde River watershed, including Big Chino Wash and its major tributaries, Partridge Creek and Walnut Creek.

In order to employ photographs by Timothy O' Sullivan and diaries by Sitgreaves, Ives, Edward Beale, and Edgar Mearns, I also included portions of the Cataract Creek and Truxton Wash watersheds, all within the elevational and latitudinal ranges of the juniper/grasslands ecotone. For the most part, I deal with records and photographs in the Utah juniper and grama grass habitats along a belt paralleling present Interstate

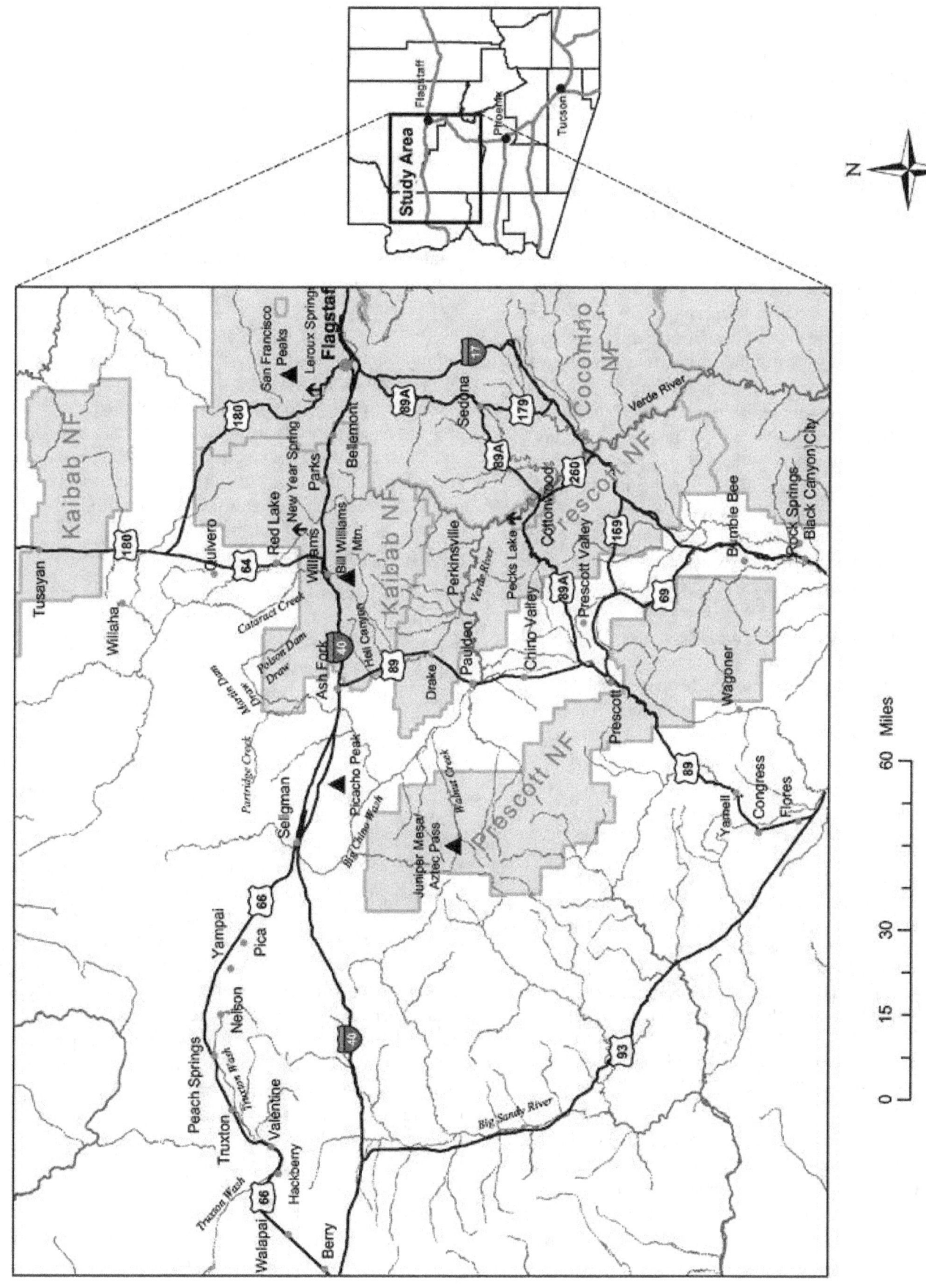

Figure 1. Study Area.

Highway 40 and reaching out approximately 30 miles to the north and south.

Prehistory

Although prehistoric man had been in the Arizona study area for at least 1,500 years (the Archaic record is unclear), no large population centers such as those at Chaco Canyon, Mesa Verde, Canyon de Chelly, or Casas Grandes existed. The walls and ruins found along the Verde River and Walnut Creek, however, show that a culture once existed here that was more centralized than the Pai tribes that were present in 1850. The Pais, had then been in the area for perhaps 200 to 300 years (Robert Euler, 1999). The influence of prehistoric Indians on vegetation may have therefore been weaker than what occurred in other parts of the Southwest.

So far, packrat midden studies (Betancourt and others 1990) have not been carried out within the upper Verde River watershed. Pollen analysis has been done at Peck's Lake (Davis and Turner 1986) near Cottonwood, Arizona, but this lies well outside of the study area and at a lower elevation. No fire history studies have been carried out within the woodlands. Faunal analyses from archaeological sites are scarce. Some insight comes from studies in other parts of the Southwest. The following quotation from Redman (1993), while not specific to our study area, represents the Central Arizona Highlands some 80 miles east (near Payson) and reflects vegetation changes in an area with similar elevations and climatic patterns:

> "...the vegetation surrounding the settlements was broadly similar to that today with several interesting differences. When Shoofly Village was first occupied, the vicinity around it contained more grassland, fewer juniper trees, and far more grass than today. During the years the site was occupied, the number of junipers remained low, some undoubtedly being cut for use as construction and as fuel. At the same time, the proportion of weedy perennials that invade disturbed land around human settlements (e.g., cheno-ams) [lambsquarters and ragweed] increased. Toward the end of Shoofly's occupation, the proportion of juniper pollen increased significantly, indicating a change in the surrounding area toward a denser woodland."

Shoofly Village, near the present site of Payson, Arizona, was occupied between A.D. 1000 and 1300. The shift toward denser woodland occurred approximately 700 years ago, long before cattle, horses, or sheep were present. It also occurred, apparently, in spite of woodcutting by the villagers.

Prehistoric climatic variation was documented for the upper Verde River through use of tree ring analysis. Nials and others (1989) suggest three periods of prehistoric rainfall: A.D. 900 to 1051, consistent rainfall; 1052 to 1196, extremes every 20 years with 1/2 high, 1/2 low; and 1197 to 1353, extremes every decade, droughts more severe. The century between 1210 and 1310 included 10 years of extremely low rainfall. Such relatively long-term changes in precipitation undoubtedly affected distribution and density of plants. Recent ecological studies (Burgess 1995) have shown, for example, that shallow-rooted grasses thrive best where the majority of rainfall comes in summer monsoon rainfall. Shrubs and trees do better where rainfall comes in the form of slow winter storms that allow moisture to penetrate deeply into the soil. Also, plants occurring at elevational limits of their range are likely to react more drastically to climatic change (Allen and Breshears 1995). The ecotone between grasslands and junipers may therefore shift over decades, according to the prevailing season of precipitation.

Anglo Settlement and Arrival of Livestock

Unlike southern Arizona and much of New Mexico, the study area was not grazed by domestic livestock during the period of Spanish settlement. Other than the relatively small herds of sheep driven by Sitgreaves and Whipple, few cattle or sheep entered the area prior to 1870. Haskett (1936), citing a U.S. Bureau of Animal Industry report Carman and others (1892) describes the route approximately along the present Santa Fe railroad as one of two major sheep driveways from New Mexico to California between 1850 and 1860. I have inspected the above report and find no mention of sheep being driven across Arizona along the 35th parallel prior to the 1870s. Haskett also cites Farrish (1915 Vol. I) as saying that Francis Aubry drove a herd of sheep across this route in the 1850s. However, Wyman (1932) makes it clear that Aubry drove sheep from Albuquerque along the southern Gila River route rather than the 35th parallel. Aubry traveled the 35th parallel on two return trips from California to New Mexico, but did not drive livestock on either trip. I have found no mention of sheep or sign of commercial sheep drives in any of the expedition diaries from the 1850s, and I believe that Haskett was wrong in identifying it as a major driveway at that time. Haskett (1935) also noted that the Beale wagon route was later used to drive cattle, but gives no dates. The earliest recorded cattle drive across the area that I found occurred in late 1870 (Grounds 1977).

Settlement of the Prescott area began with arrival of the Walker and Weaver Parties. These parties were quickly followed by the U.S. military, a territorial government, and settlers bringing livestock (Henson 1965). While some efforts at open range ranching occurred as early as 1864, a successful range livestock industry did not become possible until at least 1874, after the Apache, Hualapai, and Yavapai Indians were subdued (Haskett 1935 and 1936; Wagoner 1952; Wilson 1995). Livestock numbers then increased during the following decade, but the market remained local, mainly military. Strong incentive for grazing large herds probably did not develop until the arrival of the railroad along the northern end of Yavapai county in 1882. This provided a means of sending animals to California markets.

Relatively large numbers of livestock (Haskett 1935 and 1936) were on the range by the early to mid 1880s, and much of the rangeland was heavily grazed during this decade. The severe drought of the 1890s caused a drastic reduction of livestock and concentrated surviving animals along waterways. The effects of such a concentration of livestock on subsequent vegetation have never been fully assessed. Distribution of animals was probably clumped due to water shortage, leaving some areas unaffected and others heavily grazed.

Historic Diaries, Journals, Reports, and Drawings

The diaries and reports of the Army Topographical Engineers provide the earliest descriptions of vegetation, so I have emphasized vegetation condition during the 1850s. Two early Spaniards, Espejo in 1583 and Farfan in 1598, entered the Verde Valley from the north, but did not penetrate the study area (Bartlett 1947). Garces passed along the north edge of the area in 1776 (Coues 1900) but said little about vegetation. Trappers and mountain men such as Ewing Young and Kit Carson had penetrated the region by 1825, but they left little written record. Three U.S. Army exploratory expeditions traversed northern Yavapai County between 1851 and 1857, led respectively by Brevet Captain Lorenzo Sitgreaves in 1851 (Sitgreaves 1853); Whipple in 1853 to 54 (Foreman 1941); and Lt. Joseph C. Ives in 1857 (Ives 1861). All were accompanied by naturalists and all left descriptions of their routes of travel. In addition, journals of F. X. Aubry, who crossed the area in 1853 and 1854 (Wyman 1932), and the wagon road survey of Edward F. Beale in 1857 (Lesley 1970), John Marion's 1870 account (Powell 1965), and Edgar Mearns unpublished

1884 diaries provide limited comments on vegetation. Joseph Walker (Adler and Wheelock 1965) crossed the area in 1853 but left no description.

The quality and quantity of information provided by the expeditions was limited for a variety of reasons. Sitgreaves traveled with pack animals and a small military escort. His expedition was vulnerable to Indian attack. Also, by the time he reached the upper Verde watershed, he was growing short on supplies. Ives began his overland explorations after what had already been an extended effort at ascending the Colorado River by boat. He then traveled with pack animals and carried limited supplies. Both Sitgreaves and Ives necessarily moved rapidly through the area. Aubry prided himself on being able to cover long distances rapidly and rarely described his routes. Beale lingered for several days in the study area, mainly because of the inability of his guide to find water, but he recorded few details regarding vegetation.

Of all of these expeditions Whipple's yielded the largest number of journals, the greatest amount of scientific information, and the best descriptions of vegetation. Benefiting from Sitgreave's earlier experience, Whipple traveled with a well-supplied wagon train. He drove livestock for food, he was accompanied by a sizeable military detachment for protection from Indians, and he had a work force from the Rio Grande. Whipple planned to explore the area in detail, and one of his main objectives was to map the poorly-known terrain between Bill Williams Mountain and the Colorado River. As a result, he spent more time in the upper Verde watershed than he did in any area of similar size along his route. At least six individuals kept journals for all or part of the trip. These included Whipple, German artist Balduin Möllhausen, physician and zoologist C. B. R. Kennerly, escort commander Lieutenant John Tidball, John P. Sherburne, and David Sloane Stanley. A second physician John Milton Bigelow served as botanist. Jules Marcou served as geologist. These scientists collected specimens, maintained field notes, and contributed to final reports of the expedition.

Joseph Christmas Ives, who later re-crossed the area with his own expedition, contributed to Whipple's final report. Möllhausen, Tidball, and A. H. Campbell made drawings along the way, but only one drawing by Tidball actually shows terrain in the study area. It does not provide much information on vegetation, and may have been modified by a lithographer before publication. When Möllhausen re-crossed the area with Ives in 1858, he left several watercolors with renditions of the vegetation (Huseman 1995), but here, too, we do not know the extent of artistic license employed in making or printing the drawings.

Photographs

The earliest known photographs for the area were taken in 1867 by Alexander Gardner. Gardner accompanied William Jackson Palmer on a private railroad survey (Babbitt 1981) and left six photographs near the Whipple route. Three were taken in the study area. Gordon and others (1992) also repeated these photographs in 1989 during a study of vegetation history. Timothy O'Sullivan, who accompanied Wheeler in 1871, took the next series of photographs in northern Arizona. O'Sullivan recorded two landscapes in the juniper-grassland habitats near the route that Sitgreaves had traversed. The five Gardner and O'Sullivan photographs were taken before the arrival of established ranches and railroads.

All subsequent photographs post-date grazing by livestock. The next landscape photographs were taken in 1911 by Fewkes (1912) in association with archaeological surveys, and King in about 1916 (Johnsen and Elson 1979), documenting range conditions for the U.S. Forest Service. I also used a 1927 photograph by Gus Pearson and a 1932 photograph by Arthur Upson, both from Rocky Mountain Forest and Range Experiment Station files.

Retracing Whipple's Route

I traveled on or near Whipple's route from Leroux Springs to Aztec Pass at the head of Walnut Creek (fig. 2). I concentrated on the area covered between December 31, 1853 and January 22, 1854, when the party was traversing piñon/juniper woodland and grasslands of the upper Verde River watershed. While on the Verde watershed, Whipple led three mounted reconnaissances to locate the best wagon route and locate water for the expedition. By making these wider sorties, he was able to explore and describe a much larger area than if he had stayed with the wagons. The first of these reconnaissance trips started on December 30, 1853 and lasted until January 6, 1854, during which Whipple rode from Leroux Springs, around the northwestern base of Bill Williams Mountain to the head of Hell Canyon, off of the Mogollon Rim's western-most point and across a rolling juniper/grassland savanna to the approximate site of present Ash Fork, then northwest into an easterly tributary of Partridge Creek. From that point he turn east to rejoin the wagons at a place he had named New Year's Spring.

His second foray was from a campsite midway along Partridge Creek, westward to Picacho Mountain, then up the center of Chino Valley to an unidentified mountain somewhere southwest of present-day Seligman. He rejoined the wagon train where it waited near the southwest base of Picacho Mountain. His final reconnaissance led southwesterly across Chino Valley, through the eastern foothills of Juniper Mesa to an unknown hillside south of Walnut Creek (called Pueblo Creek by Whipple; see Appendix B for current names of features mentioned in historic documents), thence back to, and up Walnut Creek to a point beyond Aztec Pass. From here, he rode back down Walnut Creek and awaited the wagon train in the general area of the present Walnut Creek Ranger Station. While crossing the Verde watershed, Whipple traveled with the wagons only seven of 26 days. As Whipple explored ahead on horseback, the wagons came up slowly behind to campsites he had located, usually associated with water. Contact with the wagons was accomplished through couriers sent back from the reconnaissance party or, less successfully, by smoke signals. Members of reconnaissance parties and the wagon train maintained diaries, so vegetation and terrain are described from the perspective of both.

I tried to retrace the reconnaissance groups and the wagons, locating as closely as possible the places the various members of the parties describe in their journals. I photographed or described these areas and key points along the routes in order to relate present day conditions with those described in 1853 to 54. In some cases, I felt fairly confident that I had climbed the same mountains party members climbed and photographed the same terrain they viewed. In other places, after several days of reading journals in the field, I still was not certain of their exact route.

To allow a better visualization of the early landscape and subsequent change, I repeated the Gardner and O'Sullivan photographs taken near the routes of the above expeditions. Gardner's photographs were taken 13 years after Whipple passed through the area; O'Sullivan's 17 years. I believe that it is safe to assume that juniper distribution or density had not yet been influenced by settlers' activities and that any significant impacts by livestock on grassland had not yet occurred when these pictures were taken. I also repeated a variety of early post-settlement photographs that happen to match particular areas traversed by Whipple or other diarists. These later photographs were taken after the grazing impacts of the 1880s and 1890s.

Photo-points that I relocated prior to 1995 were recorded on topographical maps (fig. 3). Point coordinates relocated after January 1, 1995 were determined with

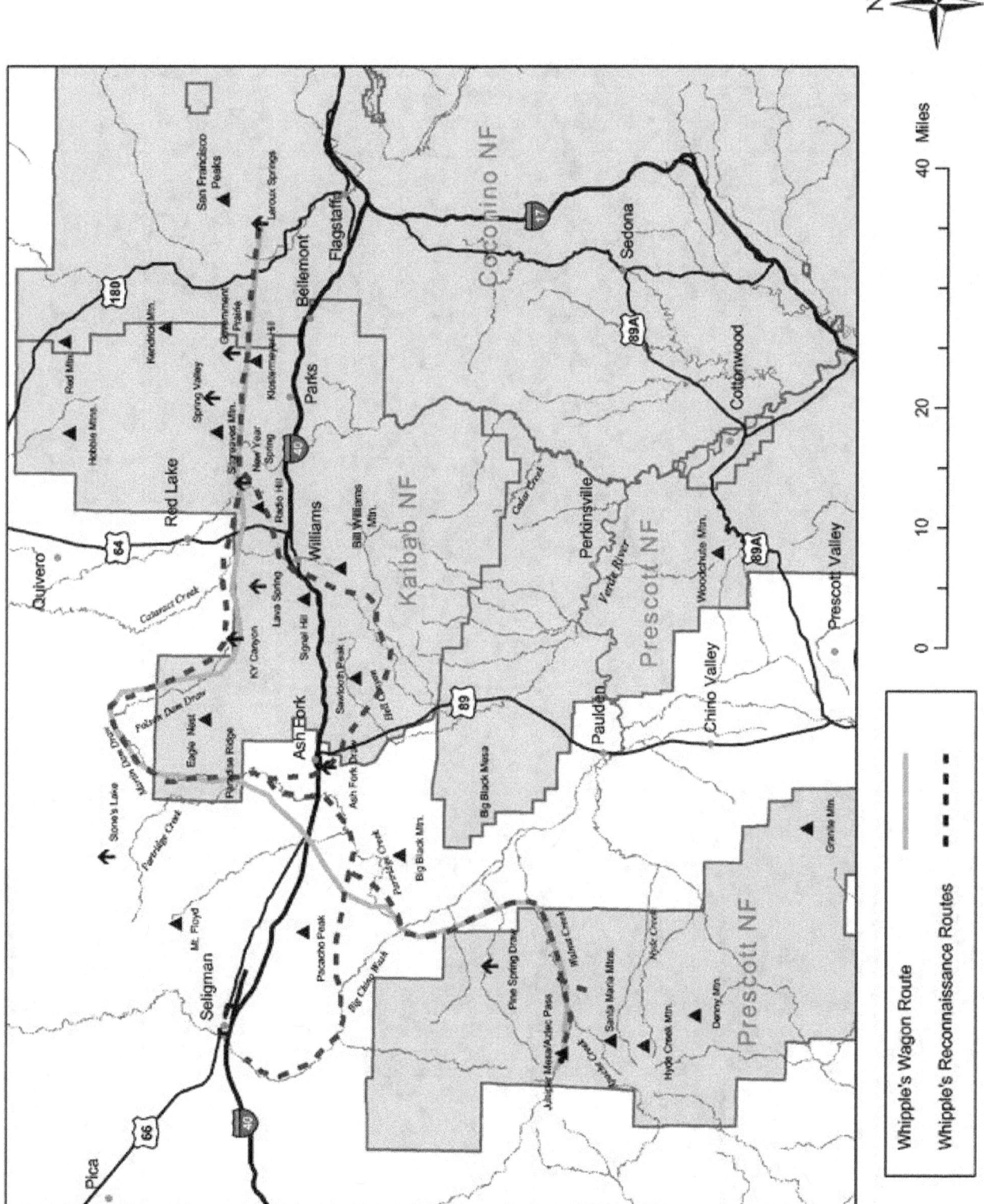

Figure 2. Whipple's reconnaissance and wagon routes between Leroux Spring and Aztec Pass.

Whipple's Wagon Route

Whipple's Reconnaissance Routes

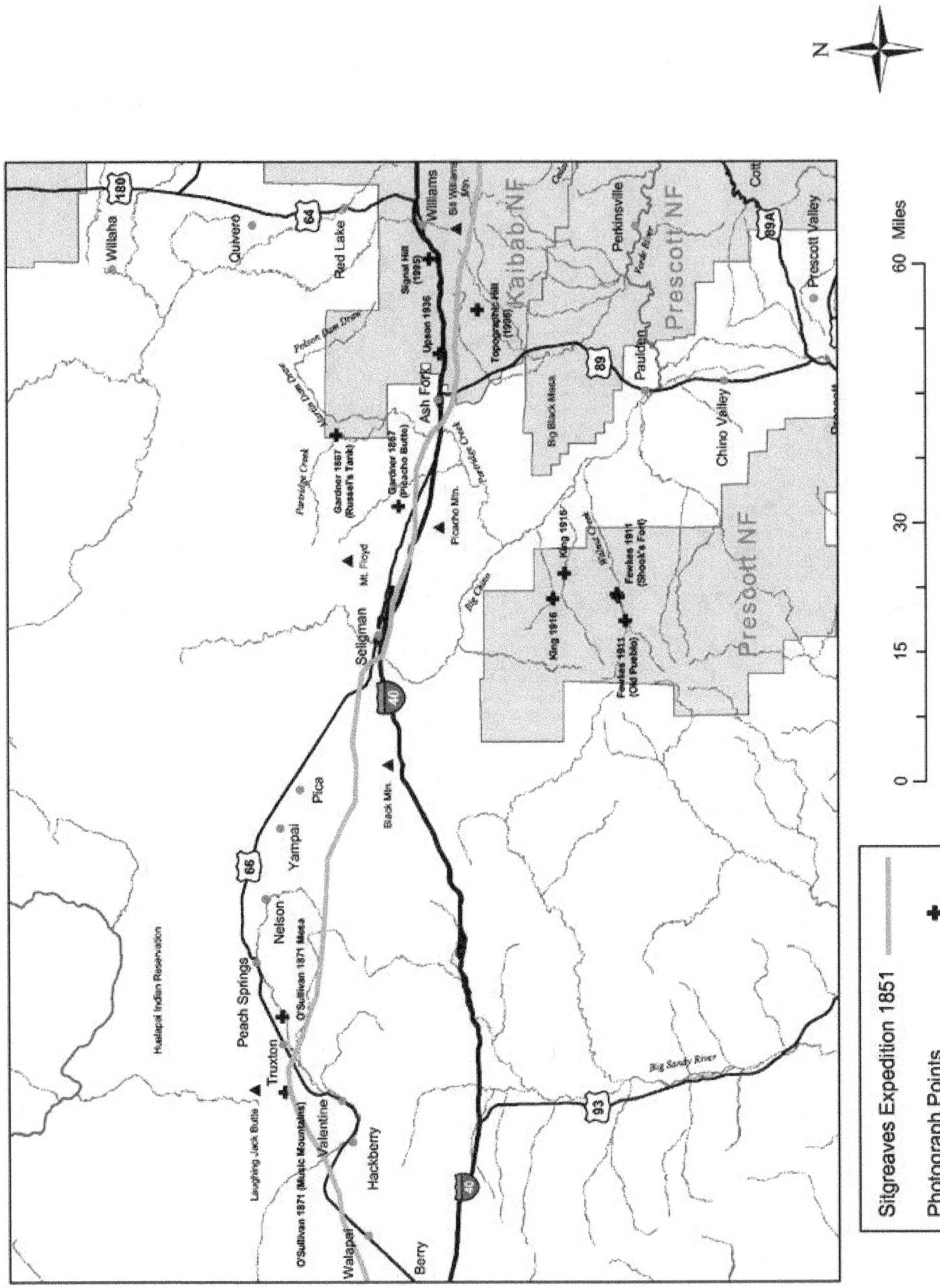

Figure 3. Location of photograph points used in this study and route of Sitgreaves' 1851 Expedition).

Sitgreaves Expedition 1851

Photograph Points

USDA Forest Service RMRS-GTR-177. 2006.

a hand-held Trimble GPS receiver (Appendix A). My GPS receiver locations were not differentially corrected so may have an error of up to 100 meters. Anyone revisiting these sites in the future can use the GPS receiver coordinates to locate the general site, but must use the photographs themselves to determine the exact photo location. The photo point for figures 4, 5, and 8 were marked with cairns and rebar driven to ground level. All of the King photographs were marked by Johnsen and Elson with steel fence posts. Other photo points used here are unmarked.

Past and Present

Ewing Young and Kit Carson

During the fall and winter of 1829 to 30, a party of trappers that included Ewing Young and Kit Carson traveled up the Verde River from its mouth and camped near its headwaters (Quaife 1966). They then headed westward across the upper Verde watershed, ultimately crossing the Colorado River and going on to the mission of San Gabriel in California. Of the upper Verde, Carson wrote:

> "Game was very scarce. After remaining three days continually on the hunt to procure the necessary supplies, we found we had killed only three deer[probably mule deer], the skins of which we took off in such a manner as to make tanks for the purpose of carrying water." For the country between present Chino Valley and Truxton, he noted that the "march was over a country, sandy, burned up, and without a drop of water."

The Sitgreaves Expedition

Sitgreaves and his physician/naturalist, S. M. Woodhouse (Sitgreaves 1853), provided the first scientific descriptions of the area. On October 25, 1851 at Camp 23, Sitgreaves traversed the country lying between present Ash Fork and Seligman, now along Interstate 40 (fig. 3). Water was a major problem during the fall of 1851, as it had been for Young and Carson in 1830. Juniper was present, but the descriptions for October 25th are sketchy. Today, much of this route has a continuous, dense juniper stand, or areas where juniper has obviously been removed.

Woodhouse writes at Camp 24 (October 26):

> "This night we made our fires of the yellow-wood, which imparts much heat and a peculiar, pleasant odor. On leaving this camp, which was on the edge of a large valley in which there was plenty of grama grass, we again entered the dense cedar timber; on leaving this, cacti and the Obione canescens [fourwing saltbush] abound."

Wallace (1984) places Camp 24 a little west of present-day Seligman, perhaps on the southern edge of Aubrey Valley. Yellow wood is undoubtedly algerita; Obione canescens, four-winged saltbush. Their use of algerita for firewood may bespeak a lack of juniper at this campsite. Certainly today, they would have had no trouble finding juniper to burn anywhere along this route. However, they could have used algerita for a single evening's fire, simply because it was easily broken and burned well. Woodhouse's comment that they "again entered the dense cedar timber" would leave one to believe that at least some dense stands had been encountered earlier.

Woodhouse continues:

> "After leaving camp 24 and passing over a plain, the first part of which was covered with [twoleaf] piñon, cedar, and yellow wood, the ground becomes more bare, producing cacti, Ephedra Americana [Mormon tea], Yucca agrifolia [yucca], Agave Americana [American century plant], and Obione canescens [fourwing saltbush]. From this valley we commenced ascending a mountain of quartz rock, on the top of which the cedars become quite thick; here is a portion of country apparently without animal life."

The granite boulder country west of present Seligman still harbors dense stands of juniper. The plain covered with Mormon tea, yucca, agave, and saltbush does not match most openings in this area today, which tend to be covered more with grama grasses. Woodhouse goes on:

> "Camp No. 25 [October 27] was in a small valley, with a little grass; on the side hills were growing cedars, yellow-wood, and *Fallugia paradoxa*.... A truly miserable country is this, where an insect can hardly exist."

> "Camp No. 26 [October 28] in the mountains, near two small springs; the vegetation is the same as in the last camp.... Following down a valley from here until within two miles of Yampai creek, there was but little change; there we found cedars, some dry grass, cacti, and a few birds; not a flower have I seen for several days."

On October 30, at present-day Truxton Springs, Sitgreaves noted:

"This rivulet, which I have called the Yampai, has its sources in three small springs; it is repeatedly lost in the ground within a distance of half a mile; after which it disappears entirely. A few willow and cotton-wood trees grow upon its banks, and green grass was seen here for the first time since leaving the San Francisco Mountains."

Woodhouse wrote at Camp number 28 [November 1]:

"…at Yampai Creek, water and grass abundant…the banks of the stream are covered by a small scrub oak, (*Q. emoryi*) several species of willow (*Salix* spp.) over which in many places are creeping grape vines, (Vitus) forming dense thickets; also a few cottonwood trees, several species of currants (Ribes), artemesia, Obione canescens, ephedra, and several varieties of cactus."

On November 2, probably in the vicinity of the present Kingman, Sitgreaves finally adds some descriptive notes:

"We kept down the valley of the Yampai some twelve miles, when, finding that its course was out of our most direct route, we diverged from it across a wide barren plain, and encamped without water, grass, or wood, the only fuel being the withered cacti with which the plain abounded."

Figure 4 was taken by Alexander Gardner 16 years after Sitgreaves passed this vicinity (fall, 1867). The photo point is north of the route Sitgreaves followed on October 25 and 26, 1851, and the view is southerly across the route. Sitgreave's description at Camp 23 represents the country west of the site in this photograph. Whipple later passed through this same area a few miles further to the south, as he traveled between Partridge Creek and Picacho Butte. The photograph will again be discussed in conjunction with his journals.

Figure 5 shows the same view on August 2, 1995 — 128 years after Gardner's photograph was taken and 144 years after Sitgreaves passed. It shows minimal change. Some of the taller grass stems are missing, and juniper is slightly more abundant. A low shrub, probably winterfat, is less abundant. The railroad that Gardner's party surveyed has been built and subsequently abandoned.

Timothy O'Sullivan, traveling with the Wheeler expedition in 1871, took two pictures in the uplands near Sitgreaves' Yampai Creek (Truxton Wash). The first, showing a grassland and flat-topped mesa (fig. 6)

is just east of the present town of Truxton. The repeat of this picture (fig. 7), taken August 23, 1995, shows minimal change in the structure of the grassland. The second O'Sullivan picture was taken northwest of Truxton in the foothills of the Music Mountains (fig. 8). The repeat of this picture (fig. 9), taken August 24, 1995, shows considerable increase in tree density, especially piñon, which was not apparent at the site in 1871. Also noteworthy are three shrub oaks in the foreground that may be the same individual plants that were present in 1871. The 1871 picture shows an even-aged stand of juniper, apparently becoming established on a previously open landscape.

Without riding through this country under the same conditions experienced by Sitgreaves and Woodhouse, it is now hard to envision it as being as harsh as they described it. The grass, even if dry, was nutritious. Water was their main problem, and they had to hurry between springs. This made it difficult to rest animals and give them time to graze. Their failure to mention pronghorns or prairie dogs is interesting, because both species are now present along the route. Both Whipple, in 1854 and Mearns, in 1884, noted pronghorns being abundant. Mearns also observed prairie dogs.

Whipple's Expedition

In early 1854, some two years and three months after Sitgreaves, Whipple's party crossed the upper Verde watershed in a more leisurely manner (Whipple 1856), exploring a different route (fig. 2), and from heights, viewed much of the country that Sitgreaves had explored. A horse and mule detail led by Whipple ranged ahead of the wagons, exploring widely and plotting the wagon route. The wagons, led by Lieutenant Ives, waited at water holes until word came from Whipple to move foreword. The wagon train functioned as support for the exploration party, carrying supplies and technical personnel. It gave Whipple the freedom to explore more widely, knowing that he had a well-supplied base coming up behind. The independent movements of the wagons and the reconnaissance parties created confusion, at times, in interpreting the journals. The wagons and pack train did not necessarily follow the same routes even on the days that they moved in tandem and ended at a common camp.

The New Years reconnaissance—Whipple's first reconnaissance into the Verde watershed began on December 30, 1853, when he led a small party away from the wagons and rode westward from Leroux Spring at the base of the San Francisco Peaks. This group included Whipple, Bigelow, A. H. Campbell,

Figure 4. 1867 photograph by Alexander Gardner taken west of present Ash Fork, Arizona. Picacho Mountain is in the distance. Courtesy of Boston Public Library.

Figure 5. 1995. Repeat of Figure 4. A few junipers have invaded and a low shrub, possibly winterfat, is less abundant. Otherwise, the site is still a relatively open grassland. Photograph by R. M. Turner.

White, and guide Antoine Leroux. They were escorted by a regular army detachment under the command of Lieutenant John Tidball. The reconnaissance party was away from the main wagon train for seven days. During this time, Whipple and his companions began to view the most important area of their expedition, and Whipple began to doubt the accuracy of the route of the Bill William's Fork shown on the map produced by Sitgreaves and Kern.

Whipple was led to believe that the Bill William's Fork arose near the base of Bill William's Mountain and flowed west to the Colorado River. Because his objective was to find a suitable route for a railroad, the idea of a long, gradual river gradient to the Colorado River was attractive. Such a drainage might provide the easiest route for laying track. While the party explored the upper Verde River watershed during the first week of January, 1854 Whipple gradually realized that Sitgreaves, Kern, and Leroux were wrong, and that the Williams Fork did not flow where he had hoped.

Alpheus Favour (1962, page 209 to 210) identified the source of Whipple's belief regarding the headwaters of the Bill Williams Fork as being an erroneous statement by Leroux while he was guiding Sitgreaves. Leroux was apparently still confused while guiding Whipple and thought that the Bill Williams Fork headed out on the west end of the Mogollon Plateau. In a sense, his confusion was fortuitous for the present study as

Figure 6. 1871. Grassland east of present Truxton, Arizona. Photograph by Timothy O'Sullivan. This photograph was taken near the route traversed by Sitgreaves in 1851.

Figure 7. 1995 repeat of Figure 6. Little change is apparent in grassland structure 124 years later. Photograph by Raymond M. Turner.

Whipple explored and described a much larger portion of the Verde River watershed than he might have had he found a river running straight to the Colorado.

On December 30, 1853 Whipple, along with Bigelow, Campbell, White, Leroux, and Tidball traveled through ponderosa pine forests and camped that night in Government Prairie, probably near the base of Klostermeyer Hill.

For December 31, Whipple's entry is:

"We continued our march through the long prairie that we crossed yesterday. It is surrounded by pine forests, and nearly enclosed by volcanic hills. The snow being from three to eight inches in depth, and covered with a hard crust, our mules, for several hours, made slow progress. Afterwards we entered a forest of pines and dwarf oaks, with large cedar trees bearing sweet berries. The snow becoming soft and less deep, we progressed more rapidly, and at 2 1/2 P. M. bivouaced upon a hillside,

Figure 8. Timothy O'Sullivan photograph of Music Mountains taken in 1871 near present Truxton, Arizona. It represents the juniper/grassland interface prior to the time that heavy permanent grazing had occurred in the area. It is possible that livestock had been herded through the area by the time this photograph was taken.

Figure 9. August, 1995 repeat of Figure 8. Woodland has grown denser 124 years since the first photograph was taken. Pinyon, not visible at all in 1871, has become a major component of the woodland. While some evidence of woodcutting is apparent in the area, it does not appear to have undergone any major juniper eradication. Note that the three turbinella oaks in the foreground may be the same shrubs that were present in 1871. Photograph by Raymond M. Turner.

where abundance of bunch grass, quite green, and cedars for shelter and for fuel, afforded a fit resting-place for the night. From the top of the hill we could distinguish the vicinity of Leroux's spring, lying due east at a distance estimated at twenty miles. The surface between is nearly level. Looking west and southwest appeared an open country, with imperfectly defined valleys, among a dense growth of cedars; but it was difficult to say in what direction was the slope. A blue mountain range some fifteen or twenty miles distant limited the view. From south to south-southwest, about ten miles from us, was Bill Williams' mountain, the highest in this vicinity. North and northwest were black volcanic hills, and a high prairie devoid of snow, and nearly destitute of trees."

Whipple's handwritten diary (unpublished, Oklahoma State Historical Society) contains additional information on the landscape and vegetation:

> "We are upon the edge of a long prairie surrounded by pine forests and enclosed by mountains and hills most of them volcanic, apparently isolated sufficiently to afford a passage between. They are covered with snow and with trees excepting the conino peaks which are solid rocks of molten lava. Below them, upon a slope of the mountain is a distinctly defined curve the "limit of pines" found by measurement to be 4169 feet above the valley of Leroux Spring. At that height no one was able to mount on account of snow but the trees seemed to be of a new species."

Thus, Whipple estimated the elevation of the timber line on San Francisco Peaks (which he was then calling "conino" peaks). He also notes that the trees higher on the mountain were of a different species than those existing near their camp. In a sense, he was prescient here, recognizing the life zones which C. Hart Merriam later named while viewing these same mountains.

Government Prairie is still an open grassland surrounded by ponderosa pine. It now has some young ponderosa pines scattered through it, suggesting that some encroachment by trees may have occurred over the past 130 years. Whipple's comment about "dwarf oaks" west of the prairie is interesting, because oak is presently scarce along that portion of his route. Whipple had been passing through stands of Gambel oak since entering New Mexico, so I have to wonder why he bothered to mention it here and if, possibly, the species was more abundant along this route in 1853 than it is now. Regarding oak, the handwritten diary states: "…Afterward we entered the forest where abounded timbers of oak and pine with large cedar trees covered with sweet berries." The word "dwarf" was added later to the published itinerary. While the Gambel oak in this immediate area is now scarce, it grows in a tree form. Relative to oaks in eastern forests, perhaps it could be considered a dwarf form. Nonetheless, the need to add the diminutive in retrospect seems odd.

Based upon the location where they were mentioned, the "sweet-berried" cedars are probably alligator-bark juniper. This species is conspicuous along this part of the route. Rocky Mountain Juniper also occurs in this vicinity, but is neither conspicuous nor large. It tends to occur only at higher elevations or on cooler sites. Dr. Bigelow (1856) had difficulty identifying the various junipers. In his report on the botany of the expedition (p. 20), he wrote:

> "On the bluffs of the Llano Estacado, and from that point west as far as the Cajon Pass, occur in many places, and sometimes in great abundance, two or three other species of cedar. Of a collection made by Dr. Woodhouse, Dr. Torrey, in the Report of an Expedition down the Zuni and Colorado Rivers, by Captain Sitgreaves, observe 'that one may be *Juniperus occidentalis*, (Hook) the second *J. tetragona*, (Schlect.), while the third is probably new' Mine are probably included in his list; and if so excellent a botanist as Dr. Torrey is in doubt in reference to the species and varieties of these plants, it would be folly in me to attempt to reduce or determine them."

I do not know the identity of the bunch grass that was present and "quite green" at this elevation in midwinter.

Dr. Andrew Wallace (unpublished manuscript) has devoted considerable time to locating the hillside where the party camped on December 31 and the spring they visited on the morning of January 1, which Whipple named New Year's Spring. Wallace presents strong evidence that the hill they climbed on December 31 is the one now called Radio Hill, located in Range 2E, Township 22N, Section 3, and that the spring may have been near the present site of Hitson Tank about a mile to the northwest in Section 4.

Radio Hill is now covered with ponderosa pine, Gambel oak, a few piñons, and a scattering of large, old alligator-bark junipers, some of which may be the same trees used by the party for shelter on New Year's Eve, 1853. The blue mountain range Whipple noted to the southwest is the combined ridges of Picacho and Mount Floyd (Sierra de la Laja). Whipple's estimate of distance was off somewhat, Floyd and Picacho both being over 30 miles direct line from Radio Hill. My camera was unable to penetrate the haze on the day I took a photograph, hence the blue mountain range barely shows (fig. 10). Whipple's description of the area to the west and southwest as having a dense growth of cedars corresponds with the view today. However, the vegetation to the northwest of Radio Hill may have changed since 1854 (fig. 11). The country he describes as nearly destitute of trees certainly now holds a significant stand of alligator-bark juniper.

Whipple's notes for January 1, 1854 say:

> "The morning was bright and clear. Upon leaving camp, we visited New Year's Spring, about a mile west.…After travelling about

Figure 10. View from Radio Hill, December 1996. Wallace (unpublished manuscript) has identified this as the hill climbed by Whipple on December 31, 1853. "*Looking west and southwest appeared an open country with imperfectly defined valleys, among a dense growth of cedars; but it was difficult to say in what direction was the slope. A blue mountain range some fifteen or twenty miles distant limited the view.*" The distant mountains are Mount Floyd, called Sierra de la Laja by Whipple. Photograph by Harley Shaw.

Figure 11. View to northwest from Radio Hill, December, 1996. Whipple's 1853 description was: "*North and northwest were black volcanic hills, and a high prairie devoid of snow, and nearly destitute of trees.*" The woodland has grown denser in this direction. The valley to the northwest of Radio Hill, while still having some open grassland, now holds a mixture of ponderosa pine, alligator barked juniper, and piñon. Photograph by Harley Shaw.

twelve miles, we spread our blankets beneath a cedar tree three miles west of Bill Williams' mountain. Good grass and timber are found here; but we have failed to reach the waters of Bill Williams' fork...."

"We are now near the trail of Capt. Sitgreaves, who passed around the southern base of Bill Williams' mountain, and thence proceeded towards the west-northwest, in the direction of Yampais creek. Lieut. Tidball has taken a sketch showing the Sierra de la Laja and Picacho, some twenty-five miles distant, between which the trail crossed. A chain of blue hills appears in the distance, and extends towards the south-southeast; its crest evidently preserving nearly the same altitude; but the descent of the valley along its foot causes the southern portion, represented in the sketch, to appear a formidable range. The drainage of the

ravines is towards Picacho, through a generally level country, containing prairies mingled with copses of piñons and cedars. The soil, being of decomposed volcanic rock, is rich; and, judging from the vegetation which covers it, must be well-watered. Captain Sitgreaves, according to Leroux, found this region to be a plain intersected by numerous and difficult ravines. The country beyond proved to be an elevated prairie, considerably broken, and nearly devoid of water and wood, forming a dreary jornada. The grass, though nutritious and abundant, was parched, indicating a long drought. The soil was so light and porous, that there appeared little chance of finding water in pools...."

"The region from the San Francisco mountain to this place contains much volcanic sand and scoriaceous rock, quickly absorbing rain and melting snow.... Pine forests, interspersed with prairies, seem to extend towards the south to the blue mountains that are just visible above the horizon. The appearance is somewhat similar to the Cross Timbers upon the Canadian. Our camp is on a dry branch of Bill Williams' fork, and according to the barometer, 400 feet below the bivouac of last night."

Whipple has modified his description of vegetation here from that in his handwritten diary. There, his only note of the appearance of vegetation says: "Pine forests interspersed with prairies extend in all directions to the furtherst limits of sight." He makes no mention of piñon or cedar. In his later report, he adds the sentence on copses of piñons and cedars, apparently because by then he had ridden through them and realized that they were not all pine forests. Based upon his diary written on site, the general appearance of the landscape has not changed much since Whipple described it.

Whipple states that they failed to reach the waters of Bill William's Fork, yet says at the end of the entry that they were camped on a dry branch of that river. I believe they encamped just west of the present town site of Williams. The hill they climbed was probably one now named on maps as Signal Hill. One source of evidence I used in locating this hill is Lieutenant Tidball's sketch (fig. 12), which apparently was erroneously labeled in Whipple's report. Rather than Picacho and Sierra de la Laja, Tidball's sketch better matches the landscape to the southwest of this hill. This shows Granite Mountain and Sullivan Buttes near the present site of Prescott, although the sketch seems magnified from the actual view (fig. 13). I climbed several of the hills in this immediate vicinity, but this location provides the only scene that approximates the angle of the sketch (which may have been embellished by a lithographer). Whipple's handwritten diary supports this conclusion, noting that Tidball's sketch is of the south end of the range that includes Juniper Mesa and the Santa Maria Mountains. From this hill, Granite Mountain appears to be an extension of that range.

The handwritten diary adds to the confusion about this sketch. In it, Whipple does not mention Tidball's sketch of "Picacho" but rather notes: "Bill Williams Mt rises behind us presenting a view correctly represented in a sketch by L. Titbald." He does not mention Picacho or Sierra de la Laja until January 3, and at that time, does not distinguish them as two mountains noting, rather: "...The Mesa Mountain which bounds the valley on the S.E. is called Sierra Tonto. South is Sierra Prieta and due west is a sugar loaf peak called Picacho Laja." Sierra Tonto, I believe is Woodchute Mountain east of Chino Valley; Sierra Prieta is Granite Mountain and

the present Sierra Prieta/Bradshaw complex (I believe Tidball actually sketched this); and Picacho Laja is Picacho Peak. When compiling his report, Whipple apparently gave the name Sierra de la Laja to Mount Floyd in retrospect. Whipple refers to the Santa Maria range when he discussed the unbroken range of hills (hidden by haze in fig. 14). Here, I suspect he is expressing his puzzlement over the route of the Bill William's fork. His view of Chino Valley, obviously running in the wrong direction to lead him easily to the Colorado, is the first hint that his expectations regarding the William's Fork may be unfounded. His description of a prairie, mingled with copses of piñon and juniper does not match the present scene, where a relatively dense stand of juniper now exists. Many of the openings across the center of the recent photograph are clearings caused by eradication of juniper during the past century in efforts to favor grasses.

Comparing Whipple's description of this area with the current photos, we see evidence that, although juniper densities have increased, the area was not devoid of junipers in 1854. Any increase seems to be a result of trees filling in spaces where the species was already present, rather than a shifting of woodland boundaries.

Leaving this campsite on January 2, Whipple describes the route for that day:

"Turning south and southeast along the channel of an arroyo, in half an hour we found pools of water. Willows growing upon the bank seemed to indicate that it was permanent, though melting snows have probably added to the usual quantity. Keeping our course three miles over a prairie which sloped from the southern base of Bill William's mountain, we again found water which supplied the train. We then followed Leroux in search of the main stream, to a point which he recognized as being near Capt. Sitgreaves' Camp no. 21. Here we saw the ravine in which the creek flowed south, and followed a branch about four miles to a point of hills, where we again encamped. The stream below us flows in a cañon 150 feet deep. Ascending a hill half a mile south, we saw an immense and beautiful valley, into which the creek enters from the mouth of the cañon about four miles distant. The valley is striped with timber and prairie, and extends from north-northwest to south-south-east. It seems to be a well-watered region, and a winter retreat of Indians, for several smokes were seen there. Upon the slopes of the hills we find in the vegetation an agreeable change from that of the higher country we left. Agave Mexicana is quite abundant. It is the beautiful American aloe, the Century plant, called in this

Figure 12. Drawing by Lt. John Tidball from "Telegraphic Hill." Apparently looking southwest toward Granite Mountain (see Figure 13).

Figure 13. Recent photograph of Granite Mountain and Sullivan Buttes as seen from Signal Hill. I believe that this is the landscape that Lt. John Tidball sketched on January 1, 1854. "*Lieut. Tidball has taken a sketch showing the Sierra de la Laja and Picacho, some twenty-five miles distant.... the descent of the valley...causes the southern portion, represented in the sketch, to appear a formidable range.*" The photograph here, taken in 1996 , is a telephoto shot framed to try to match Lt. Tidball's sketch. The sketch resembles this landscape and bears no resemblance at all to either Picacho Mountain, Mount Floyd, or Bill Williams Mountain as seen from this point. The buildings to the left are the Headquarters of the Hat Ranch. The clearing and drainage running down and to the right of these buildings is the route, I believe, the party traversed on the morning of January 2, 1854 in their futile search for the headwaters of the Bill Williams River. Photograph by Harley Shaw.

Figure 14. Recent photograph of Picacho and Mount Floyd (Whipple's Sierra de la Laja) viewed from Signal Hill. Whipple notes that Sitgreave's route led between these two mountains, as did later the Beale Wagon Road, the Santa Fe Railroad, U.S. Highway 66, and Interstate 40. He wrote: "*The drainage of the ravines is towards Picacho, through a generally level country, containing prairies mingled with copses of pinyons and cedars.*" The vegetation would better be described today as an extended woodland with scattered openings. Most of the openings are areas that have been cleared of juniper by the U.S. Forest Service. Photograph by Harley Shaw.

country Mezcal. The Apaches roast it for food; Mexicans distil from it a spiritous liquor."

The arroyo they followed upon leaving this camp was probably the Pine Springs drainage, and the prairie through which they passed the next morning would be in the vicinity of present-day Hat Ranch. This prairie slopes more from the westerly base of the mountain. The stream (either Hell Canyon or Devil Dog—they parallel each other in this vicinity) runs more westerly than southerly. Actually, the handwritten diary says: "Here we saw the line of river flowing S.W...." The W is at the edge of the diary page and was apparently inadvertently dropped when the itinerary was published.

I tried, but failed, to match Whipple's directions with terrain features other than the above . By assuming he was loosely designating directions (calling northwest, west and southwest, south) the route followed on January 2 makes sense and places their evening camp on somewhere near the present Nagiller Tank on the Kaibab National Forest. This matches with coordinates, provided by Tidball in his journal, for the hilltop they climbed the morning of January 3 (quoted below).

On January 3, the party climbed a hill, then dropped off of the west end of the Mogollon Rim, heading northwest. In his entry for this day, Whipple first acknowledges his suspicion that the drainage they were camped on was not Bill William's Fork. In fact, his decision to leave this drainage suggests that he was already abandoning it as a possible route and was planning to explore gentler terrain to the north. He realizes that he cannot take the wagons off of the rim this far south. He notes:

"A mile west from our bivouac No. 4, we ascended a ridge called Topographical hill, where we had a view still more extensive than noted yesterday. We can now trace the great valley, as well as the western ridge of mountains which bounds it, far towards the north-northwest. A mesa mountain towards the southeast has been named Sierra Tonto. South-southwest is the Sierra Prieta, with indications of passes upon both sides of it. From thence, northerly extends a range with a snowy peak near the center . Nearly west is seen Picacho.' Intervening is a low ridge, covered with a dense growth of dark cedars and piñons, which we call the "Black Forest." This seems to divide the drainage of the valley—one system of streams flowing south-southeast to Rio Verde; the other towards the west and south-west, probably to the Colorado. That upon which we encamped belongs to the first system, and therefore may

Figure 15. On January 3, Whipple described this landscape, looking westward across the present site of Drake as "*a low ridge, covered with a dense growth of dark cedars and pinyons which we call 'the Black Forest'.*" With the exception of areas cleared by the U.S. Forest Service treatments at the right, this view is now probably similar to what Whipple observed in 1854. Photograph by Harley Shaw.

not be Bill William's fork, as at first supposed. At all events, it passes far towards the south. Our bivouac No. 3 was upon a branch which appeared to flow westerly, more in the direction of our route. Therefore, to explore it, we took a course north 70 degrees west, descended into the valley, and, after travelling about ten miles, encamped upon a creek where were large pools of water. Small Alamos [cottonwood] and willows cover the banks. Grama-grass is abundant in the vicinity. We now seem to be below the region of pines, and of the sweet-berried cedars. Red cedar [juniper] is, however, abundant; larger and finer than before seen. There are also numerous piñons with esculent nuts, affording food for wild beasts as well as for Indians. We have seen today black-tailed deer [mule deer], rabbits [cottontails or California jackrabbits], and quails [Gambel's quail]; also footprints of many antelope [pronghorn] and bears."

I wonder about the source of the name of Topographical Hill, as well as the source for other mountains. Whipple often writes as if their names were known, but I suspect the party assigned most of them. Topographical Hill has no name on present-day maps. The handwritten diary does not mention this name, so it was apparently given to the hill later, during the compiling of the published itinerary.

The mesa to the south (Sierra Tonto) is the Woodchute/ Mingus Mountain complex; the range to the west was undoubtedly the Santa Maria Mountains, where the snowy peak is probably either Hyde Mountain or Denny Mountain. The ridge of the Black Forest (fig. 15) is now called Big Black Mesa. It lies along the northeast side of Chino Valley, running southeast from Picacho Peak. Its name is significant here as it tells us that junipers were noticeably dense on that ridge in 1854. Both Whipple, and later Möllhausen, mentioned it as a significant feature.

On this day, the party drops out of the ponderosa pine vegetation and alligator–bark juniper and enters the elevations of predominantly Utah juniper. Their route off of the plateau passed just south of the small butte now named Sawtooth Peak, thence west and slightly north across rolling terrain. They camped that night on Ash Fork, a tributary of Partridge Creek, not far from the site of the present-day town of Ash Fork. Whipple remarks again on the abundance of juniper along their route. His note that the juniper was larger and finer than seen before is significant. The junipers in the area today are mostly young or mid-aged—regrowth, no doubt from fuelwooding and juniper control efforts over the past 100 years. Many large, old stumps, remains of the earlier mature stands, are scattered through the area. The handwritten diary stated: "For fuel it is excellent and even for railway ties it is doubtful whether this country west of the Delnorte can furnish anything superior." Few, if any of the junipers in this area today could be considered large enough to provide ties. The large trees were apparently harvested quickly after the Anglo arrival.

By calling these trees larger and finer, I suspect Whipple was comparing them with shaggy-barked junipers he had observed east of the San Francisco Peaks. Much of the juniper in that region is one-seed juniper, which is difficult to distinguish from Utah juniper but tends not to have large, single trunks. I find it hard to believe that he was comparing the trees near Ash Fork with the alligator juniper at higher elevations. That species has a distinctive bark and consistently produces massive trunks. Many large, old alligator junipers are present today in the region Whipple traversed before descending to Ash Fork and were undoubtedly present then.

Along the drainage where they camped on January 3, he notes: "Small alamos and willows cover the banks." I found neither cottonwoods nor willows in this area. A few small Arizona ash are the only riparian vegetation now present.

Lieutenant John Tidball's journal (typed manuscript, University of Arizona Library) becomes available on January 3. His is the only additional journal covering this reconnaissance mission. For this day, Tidball notes:

"Travelled about 10 m. W. N. W. First ascended for a mile up the westerly base of the ravine upon which we encamped to the top of a high hill or mountain from which we could see the whole country round for 50 mi. From the West to the S. E. of us extended ranges of mountains: apparently three running somewhat parallel to each other the nearest about 30 mi. off. The intervening space between them and us was a gently rolling country covered to a great degree with cedars and cut with many ravines."

In this entry, Tidball notes that the country before them is covered with juniper, but he does not consider it dense. It seems that the distribution of juniper was similar in 1854 to what it is today, although the density may have increased. As mentioned above, based upon Whipple's note that the red cedars near the present Ash Fork draw were "larger and finer" than previously seen, we can conclude that at least some of the juniper stand here was mature woodland.

In a recently-discovered heretofore unpublished description (Tidball, 2004) of the trip, Tidball notes:

"A species of cedar, hardly worthy the name of tree, is found in most localities, and frequently gives the landscape the appearance of an old apple orchard. The wood of these cedars is extremely brittle; a slight wrench brings off the stoutest limb, and axes are not required in obtaining fuel." Later, in describing the January 1 drawing, he wrote: "In looking southward from the San Francisco plateau the lay of the country—gradually sloping downwards—brings the scrub cedars into such position as to cut off from view the wide intervals between them: thus giving the landscape an appearance of a dense forest, the dark hue of which suggested the name Black Forest.' It is in reality no forest at all."

In his diary, Tidball continued on January 3:

"Bill Williams Mt. bore N. 70 degrees E. and was about 15 mi. off. The top of San F. could not be seen. From this hill we took a W. N. W. course, winding down through the ravines upon the side of the hill, which upon this side was about 15 hundred feet. The descent was exceedingly difficult and hard upon the mules from the hard angular, volcanic stones of which the mountains are composed. We then travelled along the dry ravines and rolling grounds to our present camp 19th which is upon a stream running westwardly, dry however except in holes. The snow, which I suppose was lighter in this long. had entirely disappeared. Grass good."

Tidball's compass bearing on Bill William's Mountain, and his note that the San Francisco Peaks were hidden, help to identify the hill they climbed the morning of the third, and I feel confident of its location. His description of the volcanic rock where they descended the rim also delineates their route in descending the west end of the Mogollon Rim. Much of the area here is made up of sandstone. The volcanic materials, however, flow to the bottom of the rim along the route depicted in figure 9.

Neither Whipple nor Tidball provide much information regarding the exact route or campsite for January 4. Nor do they describe vegetation. Whipple notes they left the basaltic soils and entered the region of sandstone. Figure 9 shows a possible route, but it is purely speculative. They more or less paralleled Partridge Creek, staying to its east. They camped somewhere near the hill now called Eagle Nest, which may have been the hill they climbed on the evening of the 4th.

The route on January 5th is even more difficult to trace, but the party ultimately turned east and headed toward New Year's Spring. Whipple notes:

"Soon the forest became so dense that, not only could we not see beyond, but could scarcely make our way through. At length, having travelled about fifteen miles, we came to the end of the range, and saw Bill Williams' mountain before us."

This is the first time they comment on difficulty in passing through the junipers. As best I can determine, they were in the vicinity of the present Paradise Ridge, either crossing it diagonally from northwest to southeast, or riding along its east slope. Emerging from trees near the southeastern end of this "range" provides a striking view of Bill Williams Mountain. Tidball also notes the denseness of the "cedars," so they were apparently a significant and extensive feature of the day's route. Actually, Whipple makes no mention of this dense forest in the original diary, so his description of vegetation for this route was added later when he was compiling the report. By that time, of course, he had led the wagons over the route, so had traversed it twice.

The entries of Whipple and Tidball for January 6th are equally vague, but their route probably ran near the present Santa Fe Railroad, a relatively gently grade that would keep the tributaries of Cataract Creek to their left. On this day, they rejoined the wagon train, which had moved forward from Leroux Springs to New Year's Spring and was awaiting their return.

The wagon train—Leroux Spring to Partridge Creek—While Whipple explored ahead, the wagon train moved from Leroux Springs to New Year's Spring and then waited for further instructions (fig. 2). During this mid-winter period, some members of the party, including Lieutenant Ives, were sick with smallpox. Ives was still convalescing when Whipple rejoined the train on January 6. Möllhausen (1858), John Sherburne (Gordon 1988), John C. Tidball (unpublished diary, University of Arizona Library), and David S. Stanley (unpublished diary, Bancroft Library) gave their accounts of this route, which Whipple had already covered.

Stanley wrote for December 31, 1853, upon leaving Leroux Spring:

> "Our road lay through a pass in the mountains, covered with a forest of lofty pines on either hand, lofty hills rising on either hand . . . . The traveling today was very laborious. The snow was deep and had a crust upon it which chafed the legs of our mules most cruelly. We, encamped after a march of nine miles, upon the south slope of a hill, it being the only place we could find grass for our half-famished mules. I ascended a high hill in our vicinity, but no promised cañon repaid me by the prospect for my toil. Rugged mountains and bare valley, covered with snow, form the only features as far as the eye can reach."

This must be somewhere in the vicinity of Government Prairie. Stanley's "promised cañon" presumably is Bill William's Fork—the drainage they hoped to descend. Klostermeyer Hill, about 9 miles from Leroux Spring,

would be a good candidate for the hill that Stanley climbed.

Stanley's entry for January 1 is brief, noting that they progressed six miles. On January 2, he notes:

> "March nine miles to-day through a pine wood and encamped upon a spring in a beautiful little valley, north of Williams Mountain. Saw many tracks of grizzly bear—killed squirrels [Abert's]."

This camp was at New Year's Spring. Whipple had sent messengers back on December 31 to lead the wagons to this point. The country approaching it is still a pine wood. The mention of grizzly bear by Stanley, also Möllhausen, is of interest. Although Whipple had passed through this area only two days before, he does not mention bear sign in any of his report. However, in his diary, on January 3, he writes: "...During our reconnaissance footracks of antelope and bear have been numerous." Whipple often caught up in his diary, recording some things in retrospect perhaps several days after he had noticed them. Thus, he probably did see bear tracks near New Year's Spring, on New Years Day, but did not get around to recording them until January 3. Grizzlies are known to hibernate, usually entering their dens by mid-November (Brown 1985, Storer and Tevis 1955). Observations of grizzlies in mid-winter are rare, even in modern studies where the animals are being radio tracked. For this party, virtually the first group of naturalists to visit the vicinity of Sitgreaves Mountain, to find large numbers of grizzlies wandering around in early January seems extremely unusual.

From Whipple's official report in the section titled Description of the Country, the area around New Year's Spring was thus described:

> "Nearly south-southwest from New Year's spring is Bill Williams mountain, about 10 miles distant, whose peaks are above 3000 feet high [here, Whipple refers to their height above the plateau]. The intermediate country has a generally level surface, divided into woodland and prairie. The hill slopes are covered with pine timber."

> "One mile east from New Year's spring there is a hill about 200 feet high, from the top of which is obtained an extensive view of the surrounding country. Towards the north and north-northwest appears an elevated plain, looking bleak, waterless and barren. It is dotted with conical hills of black and volcanic rock. In a west-northwest direction, a broad, open valley, dark with the foliage of cedar forests,

extends to the mountains of La Laja, and for some distance is bounded upon the southwest by a low range of hills covered with trees excellent for timber. Towards the south-southwest lies the volcanic pile of mountains called "Bill Williams", west of which is a succession of valleys and plains extending about 30 miles from New Year's spring to a conspicuous peak known as Picacho. This is the southern terminus of the range of La Laja; and at its base Partridge Creek, which drains the intermediate country and empties into Val de China. The triangular space included between New Year's spring, Bill Williams Mountain, and Picacho, has the appearance of a vast plain sloping gently to the southwest; examined more minutely, it is dotted with small hills and traversed by valleys, which in a few places are contracted, and enclosed by low walls forming canyons. There is good pine timber in the vicinity of New Year's spring and also in the region of Bill Williams' mountain. East of Val de China lies an extensive tract covered with large cedars and pinions, forming the so-called Black Forest."

"New Year's spring, at Camp 94, is at the head of one of the branches of Park valley. It is surrounded by a grove of pine trees, from 125 to 150 feet in height. Leaving the spring, we ascend the low prairie ridge and take a westerly course over a surface that, at a distance appears level, but is found to be considerably broken by ravines, some of them 30- to 50-feet in depth. The first contained pools of water. Station 1 [station numbers apparently refer to observation points used by the geologist, Marcou] is in Park Valley which, covered with cedar trees, extends like a broad plain towards the northwest, with the view uninterrupted almost to the horizon."

These various quotations from both the reconnaissance party and from the members of the wagon train, which camped at New Year's Spring for about six days, combine to leave an impression that the area has not changed much in aerial appearance over the past 130 years. It still supports stands of ponderosa pine mixed with alligator-bark juniper and piñons. We can judge little about age and distribution of pines from the journals, beyond the fact that a stand of large ponderosa pines apparently surrounded New Year's Spring. The country around Spring Valley may have been somewhat more open than it is now, but Whipple's comment that Park Valley was covered with cedar trees seems to contradict his earlier description in the itinerary.

Describing the camp and area northeast of Bill Williams Mountain, where the main party awaited Whipple during his reconnaissance to the west (approximately January 1 to January 8), Möllhausen wrote:

"We had now for a considerable extent the same scenery, the same rough ground, the same deep ravines, lava fields, and volcanic hills. Here and there we saw solitary specimens of the black-tailed deer and antelope, and more frequently wolves and cayotas announced their presence by howling and chattering as they prowled around us in the scanty cedar woods; there was a dreary character in the whole landscape that gave us little hope of any better pasture for our cattle…"

Janknecht (personal email communication) notes that a more accurate interpretation would be "better terrain for our animals," which might refer to the condition of the route over which they were passing. Möllhausen's use of the word "scanty" in describing the cedar woods could be significant. In most places where juniper exists today, it is relatively dense. However, he may have been referring to the size of the trees rather than their density.

In his Report on the Botany of the Trip, Dr. Bigelow provided an overview of the area:

"On the slopes east and south of San Francisco mountain, looking into this valley and also westwardly, are vast forests of piñon, intermingled with cedars, perfectly black in the distance, by their density. From elevated points near the southern base of Bill Williams' mountain we had extensive and beautiful views of these forests, which extended southwestwardly, apparently some fifteen or twenty miles. This one we denominated the Black Forest'."

Dr. Kennerly was the frequent companion of Möllhausen, yet his description (Kennerly 1856) of the same area contrasts somewhat with that of his friend:

"A few short marches through dense pine forests and the deep snow brought us near Mount Sitgreaves, from the base of which stretched beautiful valleys, covered with grass and dotted by clumps of cedars. This mountain had been, apparently before the falling of the snow, the peculiar home of grizzly bears; but the cold and want of food had caused them all to go in search of other quarters. The number of trails of this animal that we found here, all leading towards the south, is almost incredible."

"From this point our journey lay, for some days, along beautiful valleys, and often through thick and dark forests of cedars...."

After rejoining the wagons at New Year's Spring, the reconnaissance party rested and worked on equipment for a day, then on January 8, they all started down the western slope of the Mogollon Rim. Their route was probably close to the present gas pipeline leading westward from Radio Hill (and Hitson Tank) to a spring they called Lava Spring. Whipple, in his handwritten diary, calls this Santo Domingo Spring, showing that names changed and evolved as the party discussed them over time. Dr. Andrew Wallace (unpublished manuscript) presents evidence that Lava Spring was approximately at the present site of Canyon Tank, some 5 miles NW of the present town of Williams. Whipple's notes for the day tell us little about the vegetation or terrain, but Stanley wrote on January 8:

"Moved this morning—a westerly course—over a country of dreadful extremes—rough and difficult. Surface of the country undulating with cañon in the traprock. Pine timber for six miles—where the character of the surface changes somewhat and the growth is scrub cedar. Encamped, after a march of ten miles, at the head of a deep and rugged canon, where water is abundant, but hard to approach. No game except a few small rabbit."

Stanley therefore documents their transition into juniper vegetation. His description generally fits the area today. His comment on "scrub cedar" suggests the juniper trees may not have been large. Through this stretch today, the uplands around Canyon Tank are covered with dense stands of alligator-bark juniper interspersed with piñon. Ponderosa pine grows along the drainages.

For January 9, leaving Lava Spring, Whipple notes:

"A dense growth of tall cedars and piñons covered the ground.... Having travelled ten miles, we encamped in the valley, near a cedar grove, where we found good grass as usual, and a patch of snow upon the hillside which supplied us with water."

In his diary, he describes the camp for January 9 as being "among fine cedars with grass...."

Tidball writes for January 9:

"Traveled 10 1/2 mi. leaving our exploring trail slightly to our right. Encamped without water, good grass, and so much cedar that it is difficult to travel through the thickets."

Stanley, January 9:

"Marched ten miles to-day, over an undulating country covered with cedar. Encamped without water. From one of the heights to-day had an extensive view, embracing San Francisco Mt., Sitgreaves, Sennrick [Kendrick?], Pineletta [Pinevita?], Bill Williams, Picacho, Black Mountain, north of puno [?] villages. Passed down a very bad hill and through a dense growth of cedar. Encamped in a pretty little valley at the mouth of a deep canon. To our north we have an extensive plain, extending north to the Colorado"

John P. Sherburne did not often mention the vegetation, but his few descriptions are revealing. On January 9, he notes: "No water in camp, plenty of wood.... Part of the road had to be cut, the timber (cedar) was so thick."

This is the stretch between Lava Springs [Canyon Tank] and Cedar Creek [Polson Dam Draw]. There is little doubt that a fairly dense woodland existed on this westerly face of the Mogollon Rim in 1854. Today, this area is an ecotone between alligator-bark juniper and Utah juniper. They were entering the general area that Whipple had earlier noted dense juniper on the reconnaissance and where Beale later mentioned difficulty passing through the area because of tree densities. Thus, it seems that somewhere in the vicinity of Polson Dam Draw and perhaps extending across what is now called Paradise Ridge, a belt of extremely dense woodland was present. Polson Dam Draw is now an open valley.

I cannot, from the journals, plot their exact route through this stretch, however I suspect that they followed close to or just north of the present railroad, perhaps leaving it at the head of KY Canyon, starting down that canyon, climbing out one side or the other (most likely the north side) then dropping over the rim of Polson Dam Draw to camp (perhaps near the mouth of KY Canyon). Wallace (unpublished manuscript) supports this route.

Whipple notes on January 10:

"We traversed the fine valley of Cedar creek, and passed westwardly over an almost inappreciable ridge into a wide ravine; which by gradual descent, led into the great basin of the Black Forest. Thence four miles south brought us to large pools of water in a rocky glen called Partridge creek. It is believed that water exists here at all seasons. Our camp ground is excellent; possessing, as usual, rich grama-grass, and large cedar trees for fuel and shelter.... Tracks of deer [mule], antelope [pronghorn], bears, and turkeys [Merriam's] are numerous."

Of this portion of the journey, Möllhausen wrote:

"After leaving Lava Creek, the next place that deserves any mention is Cedar Creek, a tolerably broad valley, richly grown on eather side with cedar woods, whence the small river or brook, which seems to contain water in the rainy season, has received its name."

Möllhausen's description of the cedar woods existing on either side of the broad valley of "Cedar Creek" is more consistent with present conditions than some of the above descriptions.

Möllhausen's description of their descent toward Partridge Creek says little about vegetation, but dwells upon the roughness of the terrain.

On January 10, Sherburne notes: "Road good—Plenty of wood, water & grass in Camp. Very little cutting to do on the march."

And Tidball on January 10:

"Travelled 13 1/2 mi. chiefly along our reconnoitering route and encamped in the cañon in which we last got water when out upon that reconnaissance. Good wagon route except strips of cedar forests. For the first few mi. our course was S. Westwardly then South down a valley and finally for a short distance E. of S. ...Good grass."

Finally Stanley's notes for January 10:

"Left camp and, after marching about three miles up a narrow valley we reached the summit, between the waters of Yampias Creek and Bill Williams fork. Here we again entered a valley and marching down it some eight miles, we crossed a ridge of lava and soon came upon the canon, supposed to the head of Williams Fork, which we entered and camped. Black-tail deer and hare were seen to-day and one deer was shot. Had fine sport late in the evening shooting the partridge of the country."

Stanley is wrong regarding the summit between "Yampias Creek and Bill William's fork." They are within the Verde River watershed on this day. The partridge referred to here are Gambel's quail.

Based upon the description of their arrival at Partridge Creek, the wagons followed Polson Dam Draw to Martin Dam Draw and then followed the route of the present road by Sandstone Tank, Little Aso Tank, and Mike Tank. Just southwest of Eagle Nest Mountain,

they turned down the broad valley toward Big Aso Tank and followed the general route of the present main road (forest road 142) until they crossed over and joined Partridge Creek somewhere in the vicinity of its juncture with Martin Dam Draw. At that point, they followed Partridge Creek for a short distance where it heads southeast to the approximate location of present Garden Tank. This route is over gentle terrain and fits the description of "marching down a wide valley." It also allows the four mile passage to the south coming into Partridge Creek as noted by Whipple and Tidball. The wagon train's first camp on Partridge Creek was near the head of the narrow basalt gorge, which starts just downstream from the present Garden Tank, and matches their description of the gorge. It is the only point along Partridge Creek with high, narrow walls on both sides.

Reconnaissance—Partridge Creek, Picacho, and Big Chino—On January 11, Whipple, again set out with a reconnaissance party, leaving the wagons at Partridge Creek:

"Following Partridge creek, nearly south, six miles, we found large pools of water at distances of a quarter mile from each other, with numerous recent Indian lodges along the banks. The ravine turned eastward, and appeared, after making a long, semi-circular bend, to follow the northern base of the Black Forest ridge towards Picacho; we therefore bivouaced under wide-spreading trees upon the banks."

In his handwritten diary for the day, Whipple stated: "Fine large cedar trees as usual furnished tents and fuel." They were not far from the place they camped on Ash Fork the evening of January 3, where Whipple had described the "red cedars" as "larger and finer than before seen." They were well below the elevations of alligator-bark juniper and cypress, so Whipple was undoubtedly describing Utah juniper.

Balduin Möllhausen accompanied Whipple on this reconnaissance and wrote his impressions of the area. For January 11, he notes (Möllhausen was off by one day throughout his report, showing events as occurring one day later than noted by the other journal-keepers):

"The bed of the river [Partridge Creek] could not, it must be owned, be called a positively good road, though comparatively with the ground we had ridden over for the last few days it might be called so. A few stunted bushes and a little grass made their appearance here and there between the clean-washed stones and boulders, but the upright, broad-leaved cactus

(Opuntia) attained its full growth in the chasms on the rocky banks."

Möllhausen's comment about cleanly washed boulders suggests a relatively open stream bed, similar to that which occurs there today. Coming out of Partridge Creek near its bend to the east, he continues:

> "...towards the west lay a plain that appeared convenient for travelling.... Closely-growing cedars, whose branches touched the ground, formed us a capital roof, and as we lay beneath their verdant screen we had a famous fire burning at our feet."

> "Leaving Partridge creek, which flows 65 degrees east, we turned towards the southwest and west over a smooth prairie, about eleven miles to the southeast base of Picacho. There finding pools of water, we again bivouaced among our favorite cedars. ...beyond is a broad smooth valley sweeping towards the south- southeast, and extending in that direction to the verge of the horizon.... The ridge of the Black Forest bounds this valley on the east."

Riding westward toward Picacho, Möllhausen says:

> "The ground was hilly and rugged, alternately bare and covered with light cedar woods...we encamped...where some scattered cedars offered us a tolerable shelter as well as fuel..."

They camped that evening near the southeast base of Picacho Mountain.

On January 13, 1854, the reconnaissance party turned up Big Chino Valley. Just east of the present Double O Ranch headquarters, in the narrows of Big Chino, Whipple wrote:

> "This is the most dreary camp-ground we have had. There is neither water nor wood. Our blankets, with saddles for pillows, have been placed in the middle of the valley, to be as far as possible from any ambitious Indians that might desire to practice archery at night from the hills. There is not a rock nor a bush near us from which a sheltered and home feeling can be derived.... The rich black loamy soil we have passed over is covered most luxuriantly with the excellent grama-grass, so often referred to as being abundant throughout this region, called by Mexicans "de china", from which the valley derives its name. It is now grazed by numerous herds of antelope and deer, and would furnish pasturage for thousands of cattle and sheep."

In this quotation, Whipple not only identifies the source for the name of Chino Valley, he also clearly states that grama grass was the dominant grass in the valley at this time.

January 14, after crossing Chino Valley, Möllhausen notes:

> "...found ourselves then at the western end of the valley, where our progress seemed to be barred by round hills and mountains almost destitute of vegetation.... Withered grass and bushes covered the bottom of the valley, which widened and narrowed as the steep hills and rocks approached or receded from one another."

Viewing the country from the camp in the narrows of Chino Valley, the same one that Whipple described as dreary, Möllhausen wrote:

> "A desolate looking table-land, cleft by deep chasms, seemed to extend in all directions; here and there a crippled-looking cedar rose out of one of the chasms, but there were no signs of life in the wilderness...."

The reconnoitering party proceeded up Big Chino Valley for another day, climbing two buttes somewhere along its west side. Whipple describes the roughness of the mountains to the west and an open prairie, probably Aubrey Valley, to the north. He makes no other mention of the vegetation. Möllhausen, riding up Big Chino Valley noted that a wooded mountain bound it to the west. This would probably be the northerly extensions of juniper mesa, an area heavily covered with trees today. They camped under a "far spreading cedar" that evening and burned cedar wood.

Whipple, January 15:

> "...we descended the broad sloping prairie to Picacho spring, where we found the main party with the train. They had been here two days, and the mules were literally rolling with sataiety in the luxuriant grass of the valley."

Whipple notes the acquisition of a bighorn sheep skull in this vicinity.

The wagon train—Partridge Creek, Picacho, and Big Chino—While the reconnaissance party was ranging ahead, the wagon train had come along behind and set up a new camp east of Picacho Mountain (fig. 2).

Sherburne, on January 12, with the wagon train at Partridge Creek, wrote:

> "...plenty of wood, water & grass.... Vegetation has already commenced along the route—a pretty good evidence that Spring is coming. The grass looks green & the bushes are shooting out. In a few weeks the country will be delightful."

And Tidball, remaining this time with the wagons, wrote of January 12:

> "Travelled 4 mi. in a S. S. W. course, upon the west side of the canon…. Road quite rough, grass good. Water in holes in the canon."

Stanley on January 12 comments:

> "…bad country covered with mal pais…. Doct. K. and myself went in search of mageng and after a lanorious [laborious?] walk of three miles or more, we found some very pretty plants…."

I have been unable to identify "mageng." They were near the mouth of the narrow basaltic gorge through which Partridge Creek flows, just northwest of the town of Ash Fork.

After traveling to the base of Picacho with the main Whipple wagon party on January 13, Sherburne notes: "…wood in vicinity scarce." He gives no further descriptions of vegetation across Chino Valley or up Pueblo Creek.

Tidball, on January 13, writes:

> "…struck S. Westerly across a fine rolling country for about 9 mi. at which we left the end of a range of hills to our left and struck a series of canons very difficult to pass and which debouche into a valley running S. E. Encamped at No. 27 without much wood in our immediate vicinity. Water in holes in canons near by. Grass pretty good."

The wagons camped on the point of a ridge overlooking the convergence of Partridge Creek with Chino Valley. This site was exposed to high winds, and the wagons were moved to a camp at the edge of Chino Valley on January 16.

Reconnaissance—Picacho to Aztec Pass—Leaving the wagons on the easterly side of Chino Valley, just south of Picacho Butte on January 16, and headed west across Chino Valley, Whipple notes:

> "The soil of the valley where crossed today proved no less fertile than it appeared from Picacho. It may be denominated a rich meadow bottom, although the surface and several water-worn channels were dry."

Whipple's description of "water-worn" channels suggests that some channel erosion existed in the valley.
On the morning of January 17, he noted:

> "At daybreak the ground was white with snow. Even our wide-spreading cedar tree under which reposed a dozen persons was penetrated…."

Riding out with Whipple, Möllhausen notes:

> "…we soon reached the dry river bed that runs from north to south through the Chino Valley; but as the water here had worn the ground more deeply than farther to the north, we did not find so convenient a passage."

Thus Möllhausen also documents channel erosion in Chino Valley.
He continues:

> "Before evening we were surrounded by cedar woods…. In thick woods where there is abundance of dry fuel, you scarcely miss a tent even in the coldest weather…."

Dr. Bigelow gave an overview of Chino Valley:

> "Between this elevated plateau [he is referring to the area northeast of Picacho Butte], extending some seventy-five miles west of Mount San Francisco, and a low range which we named the Aztec mountains [Santa Maria Mountains], there is a wide valley, (about eighteen miles by the diagonal path in which we crossed it) averaging some ten or fifteen miles in width. It is so densely covered with the best grama grass, that we named it Val de China."

> "The hills bordering this valley, especially on the west are densely covered with cedars, spruces, oaks, etc., which are sufficiently abundant to serve all the purposes of agriculture, domestic economy, and railroads."

Bigelow was in error regarding the presence of spruce at these elevations. He may have been referring to Douglas fir. He continues:

> "Besides the trees already mentioned, we have here two or three species of cedars; one with a large, sweet, edible berry. In times of great scarcity of food, I believe nearly every animal in the region resorts to this fruit. *Pinus edulis* (piñon) grows in great abundance nearly the whole length of this district. The highlands which form spurs to the San Francisco, Bill Williams and Sitgreaves mountains are covered with these trees; their deep green foliage giving the forests a peculiarly dark and sombre aspect, forming a strong contrast with the surrounding…grassy plains."

On January 17 the party struck the drainage now named Pine Springs Draw, although they called it Turkey Creek at the time. Whipple notes:

> "Its banks were lined with rushes, and a basin-like valley was covered with a thick growth of timber—cottonwood, walnut [Arizona], and ash [Arizona mountain]. A large flock of

turkeys [Merriam's] was hunted in the grove, and one killed."

Möllhausen provides a more graphic description of this site:

"...we had not gone many miles before our attention was powerfully atracted by a row of cottonwood trees; and on coming nearer we discovered the dry bed of a stream that appeared to proceed from the mountains. Some closely-growing willows that we saw in a ravine led us to infer the neighbourhood of water; and we accordingly turned the steps of our mules in that direction."

"As we rode through the long withered grass that covered an opening in the wood, we suddenly came in sight of a numerous flock of wild turkeys, which, startled at our ap-proach, were running at a great rate towards a hiding-place. The shots fired among them were eminently successful; but when several of them fell, the rest spread their wings and flew away as fast as they could. The birds killed had fallen in the neighborhood of water that gushed out of the ground over an area of some acres in extent, and turned it into a kind of marsh, with occassional pools; only at one place did it flow bright and clear, towards the above-mentioned bed, and was there lost again after a short course."

I suspect this site was where Ciénega Springs Draw and Pine Springs Draw run together. A voluminous spring still exists further up Ciénega Springs Draw. This spring has been diverted for agricultural purposes and no longer runs directly down the canyon. A dry, barren flat occupies this site at present.

Going southwest, they encountered Walnut Creek. Whipple writes:

"Above was a wide bottom-land, bearing faint traces of former cultivation, although now partly covered with a beautiful grove of ash trees. Below, timber of walnut [Arizona] and oak fringed the stream, rendering the site a pleas-ant spot for a settlement.... Proceeding to the bottom, with some difficulty we made our way through rank grass and thick willows."

In his handwritten diary for January 17, Whipple noted:

"...Above appeared a large forest of ash [Arizona mountain] trees. Walnut [Arizona] oak and cedar lined the banks." For January 19, Whipple's diary further described the valley: "Above the Pueblo is a siennega [ciénega] surounded by a beautiful grove of ash [Arizona mountain] trees."

They climbed a ridge between two running streams, apparently Walnut Creek and Apache Creek, then explored southward into wild and rough country. They camped somewhere on the slopes of Mount Hyde on the evening of the 17th. On the 18th, they returned to Walnut Creek and explored westward along it. Whipple, January 18, says:

"...we camped near the headwaters of the [Pueblo] creek, where grass and wood were abundant.... Turkeys [Merriam's] and deer [mule deer] have been plenty since leaving Picacho."

Of the country around Pueblo (now Walnut) Creek, Möllhausen wrote:

"It was not, however, the grand forest such as may be seen more to the East, nor the dreary deserts characteristic of this mountain chain; but low cedars and scattered oaks and pines, growing as irregularly as if they had been flung there at random among fantastically formed rocks, and masses of rolled stones, that had much the appearance of masonry."

On January 19, the party crossed the pass at the head of Walnut Creek and rode a few miles westward, finally reaching the headwaters of the long-sought Bill Williams Fork. Weather and short rations turned them back to the head of Walnut Creek, where they once again camped just below the pass. On January 20, they returned to the juncture of Apache Creek and Walnut Creek and set up camp to await the arrival of the wagons.

Möllhausen, on January 20 (his journal date—still trailing other journals by one day) describes the valley further:

"The many windings of the stream, and the small lakes, marshes, and islets formed by it, delayed us a good deal; but we got at last upon firmer ground, where, if we only avoided the thick parts of the wood, there seemed likely to be little difficulty in getting the waggons through."
But further upstream, "The hindrances to the progress of waggons appeared to be almost insurmountable; trees would have to be felled and hills cut through...."

The wagon train—Picacho to Pueblo Creek—The wagons, upon seeing smoke from Whipple, moved out on January 19. Their route was similar to the recon-naissance party. Tidball, crossing Chino Valley with the wagons notes:

"Travelled in a S. 20 degrees W. direction across the valley to the westward of our camp. 8 mi. and encamped in a sheltered spot among the cedars…. Good grass, no water. A messenger arrived from the advanced party stating that to the west of S. of us were two running creeks beside a small lagoon and other water."

They camped in the same juniper grove that the reconnaissance party had used two evenings before. The next day, they proceeded southward and, after a short but rough excursion up the wrong canyon, where they disabled a wagon beyond repair, they reached the ciénega in "Turkey Creek" (Pine Springs Draw). Tidball notes on the 20th:

"Travelled 10 mi. S. 25 degrees W. among the hills upon the Western side of the valley which we crossed the day before. Road pretty good but much obstructed by cedars and pinons and several bad aroyoes. Volcanic rocks have entirely disappeared since we left the eastern side of the valley. Carb. limestone and N. R. Sand. Encamped at a small running rivulet proceeding from a number of springs among the hills, and running from W. to E. with tall cotton wood trees about the springs grass good but covered with snow…"

Dr. Bigelow recorded his impressions of the creeks in this area in his report:

"Along the banks of Turkey creek, Pueblo creek, and the streams which we first passed after crossing Aztec Pass, we observed large quantities of willows, which is rather an unusual occurrence in this country…."

And Dr. Kennerly provided one of his few descriptions:

"After leaving the Chino Valley, we entered again the cedar forests, where we found wild turkeys once more very abundant, frequenting, for the most part, the neighborhood of the little brooks that we found in this region, and feeding upon the berries of the rough-barked and other species of cedar."

On January 21, Tidball writes at Walnut Creek:

"Travelled S. 7 mi. and joined the reconnoitering party upon a stream of considerable size and encamped with plenty of wood and grass. The stream runs from S. W. to N. E. From all appearances it is permanent at all seasons and has upon its banks willows, cottonwood, ash [Arizona mountain], oak and walnut [Arizona] trees."

Stanley on January 21 notes: "Black-tail deer and turkeys abundant. Pueblos, deserted, numerous on the high hills adjoining this creek…." Several of these prehistoric pueblos, resembling "forts," have been recorded by archaeologists. They were built ca. AD 1200-1300 by Indians of the Prescott Tradition (R. Euler, 1999, pers. comm.).

On January 21, Whipple summarized his impressions of the area:

"We are in the pleasantist region we have seen since leaving Choctaw territory. Here are clear rivulets, with fertile valleys and fine forest trees. The wide belt of country that borders the Black Forest, and probably extends along the Rio Verde to the Salinas and Rio Gila, bears every indication of being able to support a large agricultural and pastoral population. The valley of Rio Verde, which we saw from the source in San Francisco mountains, is magnificently wooded with firs and oaks, affording excellent timber. Ancient ruins are said by trappers to be scattered over its whole length to the confluence with Rio Salinas. We therefore seem to have skirted the northern boundary of a country once populous, and worth of becoming so again."

Whipple's description of the Valley of Rio Verde being wooded with firs is, of course, wrong. The summarization from the published itinerary, above, should be compared with his entry in the diary:

"This stream is the most beautiful yet found in New Mexico; so limpid are its waters, so thick and luxuriant the carpet of grama upon its valley and hills so inviting are its forests of ash and walnut. Here as elsewhere the hills and even the mountains are covered with cedars; generally of great size and beauty. Their trunks are from one to three feet in diameter and six feet from the ground immense branches put forth in all directions affording comfortable shelter from wintry winds and charming retreats from summers sultry sun. These branches are of a size sufficient to make good railway ties and the forests we have seen may afford an abundant supply. For fuel dry cedar can scarcely be excelled. It has everywhere been plentiful since we left pine forests at New Years springs."

Thus the reference to firs was added to the published itinerary later.

Whipple's use of the name Rio Verde is of interest. At no place in the diary does the name Rio Verde appear, at least not while the party was in the Verde River watershed. Sometime after the completion of Whipple's exploration, but before the Itinerary was published, Whipple began to use Verde. Prior to this time, this river was called the San Francisco, and Leroux, on his return trip across this country in May, 1854, continues to call it the San Francisco. Another river, heading out near Luna, New Mexico, and feeding into the Gila River now has the name of San Francisco River.

Everyone together—up Pueblo Creek and over Aztec Pass—On January 22, Tidball wrote:

> "Travelled 7 mi up the stream that we encamped on last night…. The mountain contracted as we ascended to a narrow ravine along which it was difficult to drag the waggins of the S. P. although almost empty and 8 mules. With a little labor it could be made quite a practicable wagon road. Encamped (camp 31) in the gorge of the mountains. G. grass."

Stanley reinforces Tidball's description of their passage up Walnut Creek:

> "Passing up the canon this morning we had the worst road we have yet had since leaving Albuquerque. After having passed up the canon for three miles, we were obliged to take to the steep sides of the mountains after upsetting nearly all the waggons, pitching down precipices and almost dragging our waggons over perpendiculars, we arrived at a place where the canon was wide enough for us to form a camp. We made in all to-day six miles. Game abounds on this creek. Skeleton of grizzly bear found in our camping ground."

Tidball, January 23: "Travelled 6 mi…. Good grass, wood, & water."

On this day, they finally passed out of the Verde River watershed and into the Bill Williams drainage.

In his journal entry for January 24th, looking back to the east from Aztec Pass, Möllhausen writes:

> "The ravine, seen from above, looked like a long strip of pine-wood inclosed on both sides by high rocks and mountains…. Even in its wintry robe, the scenery was beautiful, but must be far more so when the now leafless cotton-wood trees that border the Pueblo Creek wear their rich spring decorations, and a bright green serpentine line winds along the tops of the dark pinewoods…."

Other Expeditions—Francis Aubry, Joseph Ives, Edward Beale, John Marion, and Edgar Mearns

It is difficult to plot Aubry's routes across the area. He traveled fast and left sketchy notes. However, one of his entries, made during 1854, is of interest. Somewhere west of the upper Big Sandy River, he notes crossing Whipple's wagon trail and says:

> "…we struck heavy and thick timber of pine, cedar, and piñon, where we were detained hours without being able to get through it and it is barely possible to pass on foot (Wyman 1932, p. 30)."

Beale (Lesley 1970), in September, 1857, traveling north of the routes taken by Whipple, Sitgreaves, and Ives, describes the countryside in the vicinity of upper Cataract Creek, northwest of Williams perhaps 25 miles:

> "Encamping in a valley among the cedar trees which cover the country here…."

He also notes at this point looking over the country to the west:

> "I am strongly tempted, however to alter my course to northwest, for to the northward appears a boundless plain."

And later:

> "This evening our road, or rather direction to the westward, led us over successive ravines, all leading to the great plain lying to the northward. Intervening, the ground was covered with a thick growth of pine and cedar trees, and apparently this country extended for a considerable distance…."

At this point, the density of junipers on a more westerly course is causing Beale to consider an alternation of his route. This dense stand of trees would be across "Cedar Creek" northeast of Ash Fork and on toward Mount Floyd, the same area that Whipple had earlier noted to hold a dense juniper stand. On his return trip (February 1, 1858), Beale also remarked on the thickness of the woodland in this vicinity and notes finding what he believes to be Whipple's wagon tracks on this day, apparently in the vicinity of Polson Dam Draw.

Of the country north of his location, Beale says: "These plains are treeless, with the exception of a very few scattered cedars of small growth." He is describing the landscape northwest of Kendrick, San Francisco, Sitgreaves and Bill Williams Mountain and south or slightly southwest of Red Butte.

Continuing northwest, he notes:

> "Cedar wood was also abundant for camp purposes on the side of the hills.... On the plain there is but very little growth of wood of any kind; once in a mile or so one sees a small cedar."

Somewhere near the east side of Cataract Canyon where it begins to drop more rapidly into the Grand Canyon, Beale notes:

> "A heavy growth of pine and cedars covered the hills in every direction, around the great cañon I have mentioned, and extended as far as we could see from the high hill we ascended."

Finally, heading southward in search of water, and camping on the north face of Mount Floyd, probably at the head of Partridge Creek, Beale notes:

> "The cedar growth here is quite heavy and abundant; I measured one tree today sixteen feet in circumference, and it was by no means the largest I saw...."

Ives (1861), in April, 1858 (fig. 16), remarked on a dense juniper stand between the general vicinity of Frazier's Well and upper Partridge Creek: "...A thick growth of cedars and pines offered occasional obstructions to the pack animals, who would get their loads tangled among the low branches."

Further along, still apparently northwest of Mount Floyd, Ives noted:

> "...The face of the country continued much the same. The trees generally intercepted the view.... At the end of ten miles of weary travel, a steep ascent brought us to the summit of a table that overlooked the country towards the south for a hundred miles. The picture was grand, but the cedars and pines kept it shut out during most of the time."

This is in the vicinity of the Aubrey Cliffs, before dropping into the flatter terrain around Rose Well. At this point, they would be looking south and southwest toward Mount Floyd. The picture that evolves is of countryside with dense clusters of juniper, some extensive in area, with relatively open country in between.

On April 25, 1858, catching up on his diary, he wrote:

> "Camp 80.... Partridge ravine widened as it was descended, til it became a beautiful valley, covered with grassy slopes and clumps of cedars. It contained neither springs or a running stream, but among the rocks along the base of the bluffs many pools were discovered. The pasturage was excellent. The place is a great resort at this season of grizzly bear, antelope [pronghorn], deer [mule], and wild turkeys, large numbers of whose tracks were seen leading to and from water holes."

Writing this, Ives had the benefit of having traversed this area twice, once in the winter and then three years later in the spring.

Möllhausen, riding with Ives, noted the poor condition of the junipers. On April 19, 1858, in the vicinity of the lagoons on the present Hualapai Reservation, he wrote:

> "The soil despite of the new snowfalls was dry and barren, small cedar forests decorated the sides of the hills, but on the plains only individual shrubs were standing and changed their shape in the distance in mirages or, dead and devoid of their green ornamentation, stuck up like the antlers of prehistoric elks."

On April 21, headed southwestward from the lagoons, he notes:

> "The character of the environment would have also reminded me of the proximity of the trail, which in 1854 I passed in the expedition of Captain Whipple, because everywhere I saw the already known change between lime- and sandstone as well as the black lava fields, which were crossed in all directions by deep gorges. The almost sole tree vegetation was formed by crippled cedars, which in places crowded into black, but thin forests or covered wide areas with their dried up, skeleton-like remains."

Finally, on April 22, entering Partridge Creek, he writes:

> "Again, we spotted the scene of a cedar forest, the trees of which all had died at the same time, namely as I assume as a result of an extended fire, which had not affected the wood, but yet removed the bark and needles."

The years of 1856 to 57 were two of the driest on record for the southwest (Swetnam 1999, personal communication). Möllhausen has mentioned dead junipers over a three-day period, suggesting extensive fires, which he assumes to have happened. His use of the word "assume" renders his statement a little puzzling. He does not claim to have seen obvious evidence of fire, but rather dead trees over a large area. Another possibility would be drought kill.

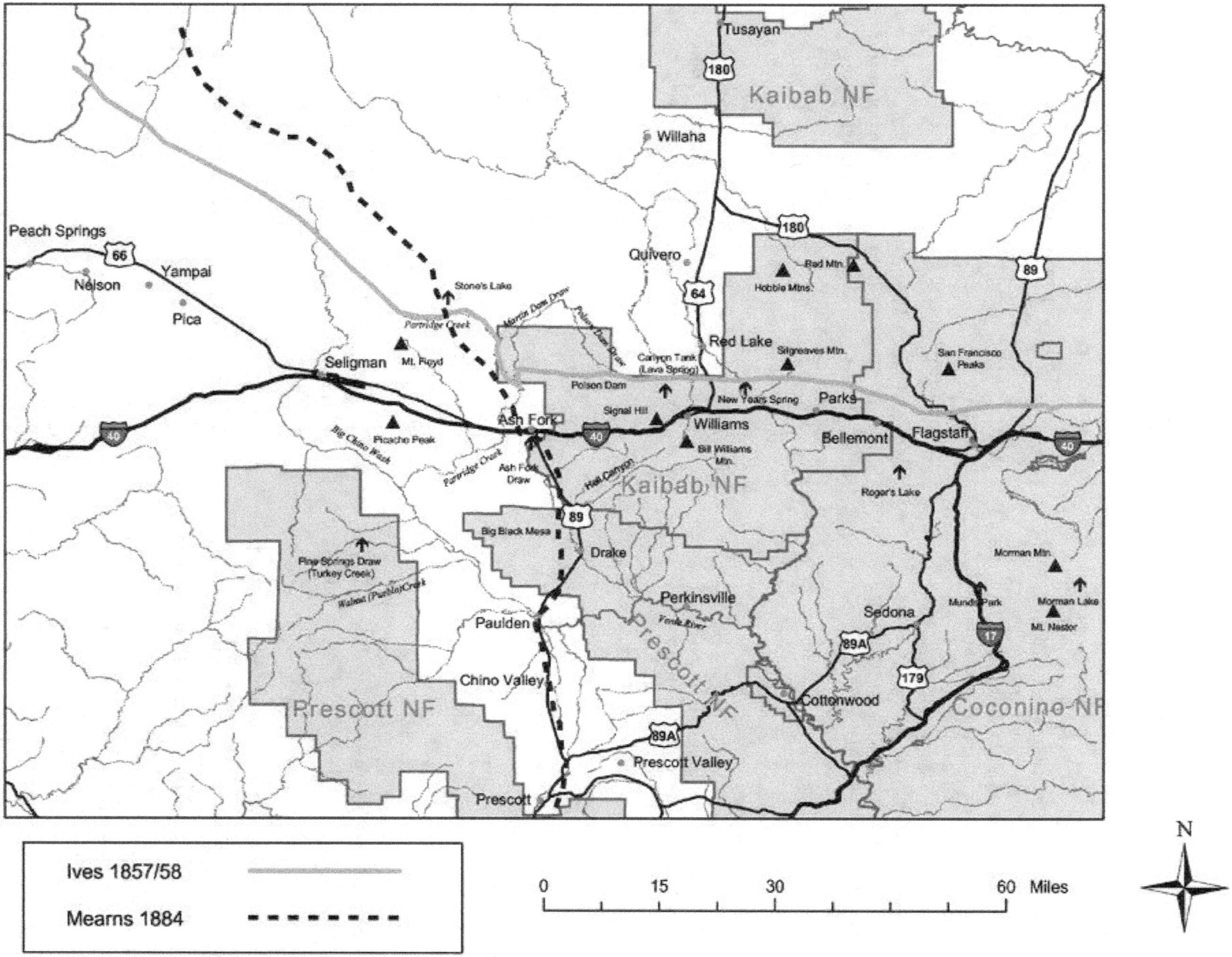

Figure 16. Approximate routes followed by Ives in 1857 (solid line) and Mearns in 1884 (broken line).

On August 30, 1870, journalist J. H. Marion (Powell, 1965) described the country between present Paulden and Drake (the area Whipple called the "Black Forest") he notes:

> "We soon reached that venerable old box in the earth known as Hell Canyon', and in going down its southern side, met with accident No. 2, ie, the upsetting of a wagon, which, luckily, caused no serious trouble, and broke nothing. After passing this fearful chasm, we drove about one mile and encamped in a beautiful grassy spot, surrounded by juniper trees, near some water tanks, around which were bones of horses, mules, and oxen, which Lo, the poor Indian had stolen and eaten. The country passed over today is admirably adapted to stock raising, grass being abundant, and water plenty in tanks in the canons. We had a splendid view of the country to the East and West, saw the great and productive Chino Valley stretching away to the West; likewise the fine large valley that stretches away to the Verde River, and which, with its thick, rich coating of green grass, its groves of junipers and cedars, pleased the eye, and filled the mind with visions of flocks and herds, which ere long, are destined to feed upon it."

This suggests more open stands of trees than exist in the area today. That livestock were not yet prevalent is apparent from Marion's "vision" of the future. Heading northeast, Marion continues:

> "Wednesday, August 31. Our road, to-day, wound through 'the Cedars', which are of good size, and cover the entire face of the country. As trap continued to be 'the formation', the reader may well believe we had a rough road, over which it was impossible to make good time…. Grass was plentiful on some portions of the hills, and scarce on others."

Marion's journal, written prior to heavy grazing, railroads, or fuelwooding, suggests that the upland around the present site of Drake, 16 years after Whipple had passed, was interspersed grassland and juniper woodland, with woodland being dense in places.

On November 6, 1884, Edgar A. Mearns (unpublished journals, Smithsonian), Post Physician for Fort Verde, rode from Banghart's Ranch near Del Rio Springs to Ash Fork, where he met General George Crook and Captain John Bourke en route to Supai (fig. 16). Coming out of Chino Valley headed north, Mearns notes:

> "The country rises by irregular undulations, until Hell Canyon is reached, bordered by cedar-clad plateaus, with a small stream flowing at the bottom. Thence to Ash Fork the road crosses a rolling country, wooded in most places with cedar and rough-barked juniper."

Going northwest from Ash Fork on November 7, 1884, Mearns describes this general area:

> "Left Ash Fork at six o'clock and marched about 22 miles to Stones Lake, a sheet of water covering from 14 to 25 acres of ground said to be 28 acres in extent. The country traversed was rolling and hilly with cedar forest, interrupted by grassy valleys and prairie-like stretches."

Mearns crossed Partridge Creek in the vicinity traversed by Whipple 30 years earlier, and presents a picture of interspersed woodlands and open valleys. This country today is virtually covered with juniper, with little open land within it. The only early photograph available for this area was taken by Alexander Gardner at Russell Tank in 1867 (fig. 21 and 22).

Mearns left a description of the landscape lying north of the Whipple route in 1884. On November 7, riding with General Crook between Ash Fork and Stones Lake, Mearns notes:

> "Left Ash Fork at six o'clock and marched about 22 miles to Stone's Lake, a sheet of water covering from 15 to 25 acres of ground, said to be 28 acres in extent. The country traversed was rolling and hilly with cedar forest, interrupted by grassy valleys and prairie-like stretches."

> "The cedars bore rather unusually large berries. Those that were ripe and dry were sweet and agreeable in flavor…."

> "A band of Antelope [pronghorn] was seen in front of the column. General Crook wounded one at long range but did not follow it. They crossed the trail right ahead of us, making a pretty picture, as they bounded through the cedar grove."

> "We camped under some large cedars beside the Lake…."

> "In the evening we built several large fires around the bases of some large, dead cedar-trees, which burned all night…."

Mearns recorded many species of waterfowl and shore birds at Stone's Lake, including herring gulls. He also mentions tracks of pronghorns, coyotes, mountain lions, and bears in the mud around the lake. Leaving Stone's Lake on November 8 and riding 12 miles to "Black Tank," he notes: "The trail lay through handsome groves of cedar . . . ." He notes killing quail "a long way from water and where cedars. . . and grass were about the only vegetation."

Synthesis

Other workers (Cooper 1960, White 1985, Covington and Moore 1992) have discussed change in the ponderosa pine forests of the Mogollon Rim. Most of these workers suggest that the presettlement forests were made up of large, older trees in more open stands. Based upon comments by Whipple, Gambel oak may have been more abundant in 1854 than it is now between Leroux Springs and Radio Hill.

Whipple described Park Valley as covered with cedars. At this elevation, the species was undoubtedly alligator-bark juniper. By the time the party reach "Lava Springs," which is believed to be in the vicinity of the present Canyon Tank, they described the area as being covered with "scrub cedar," still alligator-bark, no doubt, but possibly a young stand. As the wagons dropped over the rim into Polson Dam Draw, the junipers became thick. At this point, they are increasingly shaggy-bark, mostly Utah juniper. All along both sides of Polson Tank draw and Martin Dam Draw were dense stands of juniper, as was apparently the case across the top of Paradise Ridge. This general area was one region where all observers noted juniper dense enough to obstruct the passage of horses or mules, and to interfere with the ability of explorers to see the countryside.

Traversing Martin Dam Draw, Whipple's wagons had to negotiate sparse strips of cedar, where little cutting was necessary for their passage. Southbound into Partridge Creek, they mention no problems with trees, but rather note the rough terrain immediately north of the point they enter Partridge Creek. The long valley they followed southward toward Partridge Creek—a continuation of Martin Dam Draw—now has stands of young juniper that would probably be too dense in places for wagons to negotiate. The party would now have to cut a wagon trail or find a longer route around juniper stands, where they apparently passed with fair ease in 1854.

On January 5, 1854, when Whipple headed easterly from the vicinity of Partridge Creek toward New Year's Spring, both he and Tidball had commented on the density of the trees, problems in seeing beyond them, and difficulty in passing through them. They were relieved when they finally broke out and could once again see Bill Williams Mountain as a landmark. This leads to the conclusion that a dense stand of juniper existed over some considerable acreage in the vicinity of the present

Paradise Ridge, Polson Dam Draw (which the party later named "Cedar Creek"), and the sloping terrain just east of Polson Dam Draw. A dense woodland exists in these areas today, except for Polson Dam Draw, which is a flat grassy drainage.

Whipple, Möllhausen, Tidball, and Bigelow all commented on the Black Forest, lying southwest of the reconnaissance route. Tidball considered its "blackness" to be a result of the angle of view from the plateau on January 3 rather than extreme density of the trees. However, the party did not enter this woodland and viewed it only from a distance. They rode along its northern edge on January 3, through an area that matched Tidball's description of a savanna. At present, a dense stand of juniper exists across much of this valley and onto the slopes of Big Black Mesa, which Whipple called "the ridge of the Black Forest." North of this Black Forest, for 10 to 15 miles south of present Ash Fork, junipers were present, but apparently older, larger, and more dispersed than now (figs. 17 to 20). In the country traversed on January 3, between Nagiller Tank and Ash Fork, Whipple noted that large, fine junipers existed. Neither he nor Tidball commented on difficulty of travel due to the trees. Both Marion and Mearns noted relatively dense stands of juniper north of Hell Canyon in 1870 and 1884.

The landscape in upper Partridge Creek and north-northwest of Mount Floyd varied between open valleys with relatively open stands of juniper around their edges. At least one extensive stand of dense juniper was present northwest of Mount Floyd. The pattern of open valleys with surrounding juniper exists today, but the density of juniper has apparently increased over much of the area (figs. 21 and 22).

The country from the point the Whipple party departed Partridge Creek to where they camped on the southeast side of Picacho Butte was apparently devoid of woodland. Whipple found enough wood on the southwestern point of the mountain to build a signal fire. The wagon train, camping on more level terrain away from the mountain, found wood scarce. Few stands of juniper exist now near the southeasterly base of Picacho, but finding firewood would not be a problem, hence the woodland has probably increased in density.

The Alexander Gardner photograph (fig. 4) taken of Picacho in 1867 near what is now the abandoned Pineveta siding on the old railroad, looks across the route traveled by Whipple and probably represents the way this prairie appeared in 1854 . It was grassland with a sparse scattering of young juniper. The stretch traversed by Whipple between Partridge Creek and Picacho Butte

Figure 17. 1928. Looking toward the "ridge of the Black Forest" from the north. Whipple's reconnaissance party would have crossed left to right through this landscape on January 3, 1854, probably just behind the butte to the left. Whipple noted large "red cedars" in this area. Some large junipers are still present along the drainages, but a young stand of trees is developing on the slopes. Photograph by Gus Pearson, USFS. Courtesy of Rocky Mountain Forest and Range Experiment Station.

Figure 18. 1995 repeat of Figure 17. An exact repeat was not possible due to presence of freeway. The open area in the foreground has grown up and been cleared since 1928. A stand of shrub oak has taken over much of the clearing. Juniper density has increased across the middle area. Photo by Harley Shaw.

has since changed little in terms of woody vegetation (fig. 5), but dense, mature junipers grow immediately north and west of the place where the Gardner photo was taken. This may also have been the case when Gardner took the 1867 picture.

Between Picacho Butte and Walnut Creek, the journals provide only sparse information regarding the woody vegetation. Stands of juniper occurred along the westerly edge of Chino Valley, but seemed to give the wagons little difficulty in passing.

Figure 19. Another photograph (1936) of same general area shown in Figures 17 and 18. Juniper density had increased since Figure 17 was taken in 1928. Photograph by Arthur Upson. Courtesy of Rocky Mountain Forest and Range Experiment Station.

Figure 20. 1995 repeat of Figure 19. The ridge in the mid-ground has filled in completely over the intervening 60 years. A cleared area shows around the base of the butte, with a new stand of shrub oak. Photograph by Harley Shaw.

Rex King photographed the general area north of Walnut Creek, along the route that the wagons took in 1916. Johnsen and Elson (1979) repeated his photographs in 1977, and we have again repeated selected photographs from this collection in 1997 (figs. 23 to 28). Based on the King photographs, junipers have increased on the ridges through this area. The flatter areas north of Walnut Creek show an interesting transition from relatively shrub-free in 1916 to stands of unknown shrub species and cactus in 1977, then back to a shrub-free condition by 1997. Johnsen and Elson noted the dominant vegetation here in 1977 was made up of blue grama, sand dropseed, groundsel, vine mesquite, and some Utah juniper.

Figure 21. 1867 photograph by Alexander Gardner. Wagon train of Palmer's railroad survey at Russel Tank on Partridge Creek near the area traversed by Whipple on his New Years reconnaissance in 1854.

Figure 22. 1995 repeat of Figure 21. Juniper and other woody vegetation have increased. Several trees were recently cut in foreground. Photograph by Raymond M. Turner.

Another significant vegetation change along this route segment is the apparent disappearance of a ciénega. I believe this was caused by diversion of a spring for irrigation of fields upstream from the area. The Ciénega Ranch, where this spring surfaces, was first occupied in the late 1860s or early 1870s. I do not know how long after settlement of the ranch the spring was diverted. The photograph by Rex King in 1916 of the flat at the convergence of Pine Springs Draw and Ciénega Springs Draw (fig. 27) shows no sign of riparian or wetland vegetation, so the area had apparently been modified well before that time. Juniper has increased considerably on the surrounding uplands since 1916 (fig. 28).

Photographs taken by J. W. Fewkes in 1911, showing the easterly points of Juniper Mesa and looking back up along Whipple's approach to Walnut Creek (figs. 29 to 31) suggest that the junipers were much less dense during the 19th century.

Alexander Gardner's photograph of the meadow just upstream from the present K4 Ranch shows an

Figure 23. 1916 Rex King picture taken near Whipple route approaching Walnut Creek and 1977 repeat by Elson and Johnsen.

Figure 24. 1997 repeat of Figure 23. Junipers increased more since 1977 than between 1916 and 1977. Photograph by Harley Shaw.

Figure 25. 1916 Rex King picture of area near Whipple's approach to Walnut Creek and 1977 repeat by Elson and Johnsen.

Figure 26. 1997 repeat of Figure 25. Junipers are slightly more dense in the flat. Shrub present in 1977 is gone. Area actually appears to be more like the 1916 photograph. Photograph by Harley Shaw.

USDA Forest Service RMRS-GTR-177. 2006.

Figure 27. 1916 photo by Rex King of Pine Springs Draw and 1977 repeat by Elson and Johnsen.

Figure 28. 1997 repeat of Figure 27. I believe this is the area that Whipple described as a cienega with willows, cottonwoods, and flowing water in 1854. Photograph by Harley Shaw.

Figure 29. 1911 photograph by J. W. Fewkes looking north from Indian Hill above Walnut Creek. Long ridge across valley is the eastern-most extension of Juniper Mesa.

Figure 30. 1997 repeat of Figure 29. Juniper has filled in spaces in foreground. Far ridge obscured from sight. Photograph by Harley Shaw.

Figure 31. Another 1997 repeat of Figure 29 taken above and behind original point to show changes in distant landscape. Juniper and shrub density has increased markedly across the valley. Photograph by Harley Shaw.

Figure 32. Alexander Gardner 1867 photograph looking up Walnut Creek from approximate site of present bridge on Williamson Valley road.

Figure 33. 1997 repeat of Figure 32. Rocks in center of photograph were removed during road and bridge construction. This is near the point Whipple entered Walnut Creek in 1854. Photograph by Raymond M. Turner.

Figure 34. J. W. Fewkes 1911 photograph of Walnut Creek, looking from site of Whipple's "old pueblo" down and across the stream. This photograph probably looks down on a place Whipple camped in Walnut Creek while waiting for the wagons to catch up.

Figure 35. 1997 repeat of Figure 34. Photograph by Harley Shaw.

area that appears to be a wet meadow (figs. 32 and 33). No cottonwoods are visible here. By this time, the canyon was receiving sporadic use as a road between Hardyville on the Colorado River and the new settlement of Prescott. Both military and civilian wagons had moved through the area, and some livestock had been driven along the drainage in addition to mules and horses. It probably was not settled or being used as permanent pasture as yet because of the continued attacks by Indians. Walnut Creek apparently was a wetland in the vicinity of the present K4 ranch and narrowed to a drainage bordered by cottonwoods higher up. It is interesting that Whipple failed to mention cottonwoods in the Walnut Creek drainage, identifying everything as ash, walnut, and willow. Tidball and Möllhausen both mentioned cottonwoods in Walnut Creek. The ciénegas are missing today, and cottonwoods have extended into the area photographed by Gardner.

Fewkes took one photograph looking down Walnut Creek from the site of Whipple's "old pueblo" (fig. 34). Quality of this photograph, taken from the report, is not good, and it is difficult to identify tree species growing along the stream channel. Cottonwoods were present in 1997 when this picture was repeated (fig. 35).

The picture that emerges of the general study area, for the mid-19th century, is one of a dry short grass prairie intermixed with stands of juniper. It may have been more savanna-like than it is now. Woodlands now seem denser, mainly on ridges in areas where they existed in 1854, but I see no evidence that they have greatly extended their range into the larger valleys, such as Big Chino.

A few stands of extremely dense juniper were present in the 1850s. The general vicinity of Polson Dam Draw, named Cedar Creek by Whipple, had dense juniper stands surrounding it. The ridge to the west of this draw and portions of upper Partridge Creek toward Mount Floyd were covered with dense juniper in some areas. The general vicinity surrounding the present site of Drake also held an extensive stand of juniper, but the diaries are equivocal about tree densities. The aerial extent of these juniper forests is difficult to determine from the diaries.

I cannot generalize further on vegetation change. This work has identified a few locations that merit further field study. Juniper population structure studies would be of value in the areas identified as historically having dense juniper stands. These should incorporate studies of harvest history. The area surrounding the site west of Ash Fork, where Gardner took the photograph

of Picacho Butte in 1867, needs further investigation. While this photograph shows little change since 1867, a possibility exists that juniper treatments have been carried out here. A better knowledge of postsettlement history of this site would be valuable.

Another area that needs scrutiny is the juncture of Ciénega Creek and Pine Springs Draw, called Turkey Creek by Whipple. This area was apparently a riparian drainage in 1854. It is now a dry flat transected by a deep gully. Here, a soils analysis to confirm or negate its past status as a wetland would be interesting.

Because of the relatively late Anglo settlement of the area, a study of fire history might be especially interesting. If the Fewkes 1911 photograph of the east point of Juniper Mesa (fig. 29) accurately represents conditions at that time, the area may have burned between 1854 and 1911. The poor quality of the photograph makes it difficult to determine if the distant slopes were truly bare or if resolution of the photograph was too poor to show trees. The Whipple wagon train noted moderate densities of juniper on the slopes where they approached Walnut Creek. The area now holds dense stands of juniper and chaparral. With the exception of Möllhausen's observation of widespread dead juniper north of Mount Floyd and along Partridge Creek in April, 1858, no other mention of possible natural or Indian-caused wildfire exists in any of the diaries. It would be interesting to attempt to confirm the occurrence of an extensive fire in the woodlands in the above area between the years of 1854 and 1858.

References

Adler, P. and W. Wheelock 1965. Walker's R. R. Routes— 1853. La Siesta Press, Glendale, California.

Allen, C. D., and D. D. Breshears. 1995. A drought-induced shift in a forest/woodland ecotone: rapid response to variation in climate (abstract). Supplement to Bulletin of the Ecological Society of America 76(2):3.

Anderson, R. S. 1989. Development of the southwestern Ponderosa Pine Forests: What do we really know. in Multiresource management of the ponderosa pine forests. U.S. D. A. Forest Service, Rocky Mountain Forest and Range Technical Report RM-185.

Arnold, J. F., D. A. Jameson, and E. H. Reid 1964. The pinyon-juniper type of Arizona: Effects of grazing, fire and tree control. U.S. Department of Agriculture, Product Research Report 84.

Babbitt, J. E. 1981. Surveyors along the 35th parallel: Alexander Gardner's photographs of northern Arizona, 1867-1868. Journal of Arizona History 22:325-348.

Bahre, C. J. 1991. A legacy of change. University of Arizona Press.

Bartlett, K. 1947. Notes upon the routes of Espejo and Farfan to the mines in the 16th century. New Mexico Historical Review. January 1943.

Betancourt, J. L., T. R. Van Devender, and P. S. Martin (eds.) 1990. Packrat middens: the last 40,000 years of biotic change. University of Arizona Press, Tucson.

Bigelow, J. M. 1856. General description of the botanical character of the country. in Reports of explorations and surveys to ascertain the most practicable and economical route for a railroad from the Mississippi River to the Pacific Ocean. U.S. House of Representatives 33rd Congress. Executive Document No. 91. Volume IV.

Brown, D. E. 1985. The Grizzly in the Southwest. University of Oklahoma Press, Norman.

Burgess, T. L. 1995. Desert grassland, mixed shrub savanna, shrub steppe, or semidesert scrub? The dilemma of coexisting growth forms. in McMclaran, M. P. and T. R. Van Devender. The Desert Grassland. University of Arizona Press. Tucson.

Carman, E. A., H. A. Heath, and J. Minto. 1892. Special report on the history and present condition of the sheep industry of the United States. United States Bureau of Animal Industry Washington, D. C.

Cooper, C. E. 1960. Changes in vegetation, structure, and growth of southwestern pine forests since white settlement. Ecological Monographs 30:129-164.

Coues, E. 1900. On the trail of a Spanish pioneer. Francis P. Harper. New York.

Covington, W. W., and M. M. Moore 1994. Southwestern ponderosa forest structure: changes since Euro-American settlement. Journal of Forestry 92:39-47.

Davis, O. K., and R. M. Turner. 1986. Palynological evidence for the historic expansion of juniper and desert shrubs in Arizona, U.S.A. Review of Palaeobotany and Palynology 49:177-193.

Euler, Robert R. 1999. [Personal communication]. Dr. Euler retired from Grand Canyon National Park as an archeologist. His comments were inserted while he was reviewing an earlier version of this manuscript. He is deceased.

Farrish, T. E. 1915. History of Arizona. Volume I. Thomas Edwin Farish. Phoenix.

Favour, A. 1962. Old Bill Williams Mountain Man. University of Oklahoma Press, Norman.

Fewkes, J. W. 1912. Antiquities of the upper Verde River and Walnut Creek valleys of Arizona. 28th annual report of the Bureau of American Ethnology.

Floyd, M. L., W. H. Romme, and D. D. Hanna. 2000. Fire history and vegetation pattern in Mesa Verde National Park, Colorado, USA. Ecological Applications 10:1666-1680.

Foreman, G. 1941. A Pathfinder in the Southwest. Univ. Okla. Press, Norman.

Gordon, B. R., G. P. Parrott, and J. B. Smith 1992. Vegetation changes in northern Arizona: The Alexander Gardner Photos. Rangelands 14:308-319.

Gordon, M. M. 1988. Through Indian Country to California: John P. Sherburne's diary of the Whipple Expedition, 1853-1854. Stanford University Press, Stanford.

Grounds, J. C. 1977. Trail Dust of the Southwest. Published by J. C. Grounds. Marysvale, UT.

Hall, S. 1934. Western Live Stock Journal. 19(12).

Haskett, Bert 1935. Early History of the cattle industry in Arizona. Arizona Historical Review VI (4):3-42.

Haskett, Bert 1936. History of the sheep industry in Arizona. Arizona Historical Review VII (3):3-49.

Hastings, J. R. and R. M. Turner 1965. The Changing Mile: an ecological study of vegetation change with time in the lower mile of an arid and semiarid region. University of Arizona Press, Tucson.

Henson, P. 1965. Founding a Wilderness Capital: Prescott, A. T. 1864. Northland Press, Flagstaff.

Huseman, B. W. 1995. Wild Rivers, Timeless Canyons: Balduin Möllhausen's watercolors of the Colorado. Amon Carter Museum, Fort Worth.

Ives, J. C. 1861. Report upon the Colorado River of the West. United States Government Printing Office. Washington.

Johnsen, T. N., Jr. 1962. One-seed juniper invasion of northern Arizona grasslands. Ecological Monographs 32(3):187-207.

Johnsen, T. N., Jr. and J. W. Elson 1979. Sixty years of change on a central Arizona grassland-juniper ecotone. USDA Science and Education Administration, Agriculture. Review and Manuals ARM-W=7/April 1979.

Kennerly, C. B. R. 1856. Report on the zoology of the expedition. in Reports of explorations and surveys to ascertain the most practicable and economical route for a railroad from the Mississippi River to the Pacific Ocean. U.S. House of Representatives 33rd Congress. Executive Document No. 91. Volume IV. Part IV.

Lesley, L. B. 1970. Uncle Sam's camels--the journal of May Humphreys Stacey supplemented by the report of Edward Fitzgerald Beale (1857-1858). The Rio Grande Press.

Mearns, A. unpublished field notes. Smithsonian.

Möllhausen, Balduin 1858. Diary of a journey from the Mississippi to the coasts of the Pacific, with a United States Government Expedition. Longman, Brown, Green, Longman, and Roberts, London. 2 volumes.

Nials, F. L., D. A. Gregory, and D. A. Graybill 1989. Salt River Streamflow and Hohokam Irrigation Systems. In The 1982-84 Excavations at Las Colinas: Environment and Subsistence, Arizona State Museum, Archaeological Series 162 (5), University of Arizona, Tucson.

Powell, D., ed. 1965. J. H. Marion's Notes of travel through the territory of Arizona. University of Arizona Press, Tucson.

Quaife, M. M. 1966. Kit Carson's Autobiography. University of Nebraska Press, Lincoln.

Redman, C. L. 1993. People of the Tonto Rim. Washington D. C.: Smithsonian Institution Press, 214 p.

Shaw, H. G. and M. L. McCroskey. 1995. Historic photographs of central Arizona grasslands and associated habitats. Sharlot Hall Museum Press, Prescott. 81pp.

Sitgreaves, L. 1853. Report of an Expedition Down the Zuni and Colorado Rivers, 1851. Senate Executive Document 59. 32nd Congress, 2nd Session, 1852-53.

Stanley, D. S. unpublished. Diary of a march from Fort Smith, Arkansas, to San Diego, California, July 24, 1853 to April 18, 1854. Typescript in the Bancroft Library, University of California, Berkeley.

Storer, T. J. and L. P. Tevis, Jr. 1955. California Grizzly. University of California Press, Berkeley.

Swetnam, T. W. and C. H. Baisan. 1996. Historical fire regime patterns in the southwestern United States since AD 1700. Pages 11-32 in C. D. Allen, editor. 1996 Fire effects in southwestern forests: proceeding of the second La Mesa fire symposium, Los Alamos, 1994 USDA Forest Service General Technical Report RM-GTR-286.

Tidball, J. C. Diary, Jan. 3-Feb. 20, 1854. Unpublished typescript. University of Arizona.

Tidball, E. J. 2004. Soldier-Artist of the Great Reconnaissance: John C. Tidball and the 35th parallel Pacific Railroad Survey. Tucson: University of Arizona Press.

Wagoner, J. J. 1952. History of the cattle industry in southern Arizona, 1540-1940. University of Arizona Social Science Bulletin No. 20. University of Arizona, Tucson.

Wallace, A. Undated. Where was New Year's Spring? Unpublished research note. Typescript. 17 pp.

Wallace, A. 1984. Across Arizona to the big Colorado: the Sitgreaves expedition of 1851. Arizona and the West 26:325-363.

Whipple, A. W. Unpublished diaries. Oklahoma State Museum, Oklahoma City.

Whipple, A. W. 1856. Report of explorations for a railway route, near the thirty-fifth parallel of north latitude, from the Mississippi River to the Pacific Ocean. Vol. 3 of Pacific Survey Reports, 33 Congress. Senate Executive Document No. 78.

White, A. S. 1985. Presettlement regeneration patterns in a southwestern ponderosa pine stand. Ecology 66:589-594.

Wilson, J. 1995. Islands in the Desert: a history of the upland areas of southeast Arizona. University of New Mexico Press, Albuquerque.

Wyman, W. D. 1932. F. X. Aubrey. New Mexico Historical Review. January.

Appendix A. Locations of Photographs

#'s	Description of Photograph and Location*	Utm E	Utm S
4-5	**1867 Gardner. Picacho Butte from vicinity of old RR E. of Ash Fork	NA	NA
6-7	**1871 O'Sullivan. Grassland and Mesa E. of Truxton AZ	12 271529	3929701
8-9	**1871 O'Sullivan. Music Mountains NE. of Truxton AZ	12 260016	3929605
10	Radio Hill looking west/southwest	12 403346	3908166
11	Radio Hill looking northwest	12 403268	3908081
12-13	Signal Hill (Whipple's "Telegraphic Hill") looking southwest. Tidball's Sketch and repeat	12 386403	3899996
14	Signal Hill looking west. Picacho	12 386403	3899996
15	"Topographic Hill" looking south/southwest	12 378494	3891335
17-18	1928 Pearson 1928. E. of Ash Fork, looking south. I-40, just NE of Monte Carlo sign	NA	NA
19-20	1936 Upson. E. of Monte Carlo interchange along old Hwy. 66	12 371922	3898426
21-22	**1867 Gardner. Russells Tank	12 359811	3917622
23-24	1916 King. Near Whipple's approach to Walnut Creek	12 334126	3878481
25-26	1916 King. Near Whipple's approach to Walnut Creek	12 334126	3878481
27-28	1916 King. Upland near Pine Springs Draw	12 337958	3876302
29-31	1911 Fewkes. Looking northwest from "Shooks Fort"	12 334615	3866936
32-33	**1867 Gardner. Looking up Walnut Creek from site near present bridge	12 334240	866694
34-35	1911 Fewkes. From "Old Pueblo" looking across Walnut Creek	12 330486	3865505

*All UTM locations were taken with a hand-held GPS and are uncorrected. They are only accurate to about 100 M. Observers would have to use original photographs to get exact location.

**Has rock cairn and buried rebar at photopoint.

Appendix B. List of Place Names (Diarist) Discussed in Text

Name in Diaries	Current Identity
Aztec Mountains	Santa Maria Mountains
Aztec Pass (Whipple)	Aztec Pass
Banghart's Ranch (Mearns)	No present name. Was located north of Del Rio Springs near present Sullivan Lake.
Bill William's Fork (Sitgreaves, Whipple)	Devil-Dog Canyon and Hell Canyon, draining from the SW slope of Bill William's Mountain, were mistakenly believed to be the upper reaches of Bill William's Fork by Sitgreaves, Leroux, and, initially, by Whipple. Whipple discovered them to be tributaries of the Verde River. The stream now called Bill William's Fork heads west of Aztec Pass and runs to the Colorado River.
Black Forest, Ridge of Black Forest	Area of dense junipers lying between "Topographical Hill" and Big Chino Valley. Encompassed an undefined area around approximate present site of Drake, Arizona. The Ridge of the Black forest is now called Big Black Mesa and lies northeast of Paulden, Arizona, along the northeast edge of Chino Valley.
Black Tank (Mearns)	Not sure
Cajon Pass (Bigelow)	
Campsite on January 13. Near creek	This was on Ash Fork, just south of the town of that name. Approximate UTM: 12 363798 X 3897010
Cedar Creek (Whipple)	Polson Dam Draw
Hillside camp, December 31, 1853 (Whipple)	Radio Hill. UTM 12 403346 X 3908166
Lava Spring (Whipple)	Canyon Creek. Approximate UTM: 12 388172 X 3906771.
Leroux Springs	Leroux Springs
Llano Estacado (Bigelow)	Llano Estacado, Texas and New Mexico
New Year Spring (Whipple)	Possibly Hitson Tank
Park Valley (Whipple)	Spring Valley
Partridge Creek (Whipple)	Partridge Creek
Picacho Laja	Picacho Mountain
Pueblo Creek (Whipple)	Walnut Creek
San Francisco River (Whipple)	Verde River. The stream now called the San Francisco River arises near Luna, New Mexico and flows southward to the Gila River.
Sierra de la Laja (Whipple)	Mount Floyd
Sierra Prieta	Granite Mountain, Sierra Prienta, Bradshaw complex
Sierra Tonto (Whipple)	Woodchute/Mingus Mountain complex
Stone's Lake (Mearns)	Stone's Lake
Telegraphic Hill. Hill climbed morning of Jan. 2, 1854 (Whipple)	Signal Hill. UTM 12 386403 X 3899996

Topographical Hill (January 3, 1854)	Now with no name. Westernmost point of Mogollon Rim, approximate UTM: 12 378494 X 3891335
Turkey Creek (Whipple, Möllhausen)	Convergence of Pine Springs Draw and Ciénega Creek. Another creek NW of these is now called Turkey Creek, but Whipple did not visit it.
Val de China (Whipple)	Big Chino Valley
Yampai Creek (Sitgreaves)	Truxton Wash or tributary

USDA Forest Service RMRS-GTR-177. 2006.

Appendix C. Scientific Names of Plants, Mammals, and Birds Mentioned in Text

Common Name	Scientific Name
Abert's squirrel	*Sciurus aberti*
Alligator bark juniper	*Juniperus deppeana*
American century plant	*Agave Americana*
Apache plume	*Fallugia paradoxa*
Arizona cypress	*Cupressus arizonica*
Arizona mountain ash	*Sorbus dumosa*
Arizona walnut	*Juglans major*
Bighorn sheep	*Ovis Canadensis*
Blue grama	*Bouteloua gracilis*
Cactus, cacti	*Opuntia* spp.
Cedar	*Juniperus* spp.
Colorado piñon, piñon, pinion	*Pinus edulis* Engelm.
Cottontail rabbit	*Sylvilagus* spp.
Cottonwood	*Populus* spp.
Coyote	*Canis latrans*
Currant	*Ribes* spp.
Douglas-fir	*Pseudotsuga menziesii*
Eastern red cedar	*Juniperus virginiana*
Elk	*Cervus elaphus*
Emory oak	*Quercus emoryi*
Fir	*Abies* spp. also, probably, *Tsudosuga menziesii*
Four-winged saltbush	*Atriplex canescens*
Gambel oak	*Quercus gambelii*
Gambel's quail	*Callipepla gambelii*
Grama grasses	*Bouteloua* spp.
Grape	*Vitis* spp.
Grizzly bear	*Ursus arctos*
Groundsel	*Packera* spp.
Hare, jackrabbit	*Lepus californicus*
Herring gull	*Larus argentatus*
Juniper	*Juniperus* spp.
Lambsquarters	*Chenopodium* spp.
Merriam's turkey, turkey, wild turkey	*Meleagris gallopavo*
Mormon tea	*Ephedra viridis*
Mountain lion, panther	*Puma concolor*
Mule deer	*Odocoileus hemionus*
Oak	*Quercus* spp.

One-seed juniper	*Juniperus monosperma*
Ponderosa pine	*Pinus ponderosa*
Prairie dog	*Cynomys* spp.
Prickly pear	*Opuntia* spp.
Pronghorn	*Antilocapra americana*
Ragweed	*Ambrosia* spp.
Redberry juniper	*Juniperus coahuilensis*
Rocky mountain juniper	*Juniperus scopulorum*
Rushes	*Juncus* spp.
Sage brush	*Artemisia* spp.
Sand dropseed	*Sporobolus cryptandrus*
Spruce	*Picea* spp.
Utah juniper	*Juniperus osteosperma*
Willow	*Salix* spp.
Winterfat	*Krascheninnikovia lanata*
Wolves	*Canis lupus*
Yellow wood, algerita	*Mahonia trifoliolata*
Yucca	*Yucca* spp.

USDA Forest Service RMRS-GTR-177. 2006.